Preventing Child Maltreatment in the U.S.

American Indian and Alaska Native Perspectives

Violence Against Women and Children

Series editor, Judy L. Postmus

Violence affects millions of women and children across the globe. Gender-based violence affects individuals, families, communities, and policies. Our new series includes books written by experts from a wide range of disciplines, including social work, sociology, health, criminal justice, education, history, and women's studies. A unique feature of the series is the collaboration between academics and community practitioners. The primary author of each book in most cases is a scholar, but at least one chapter is written by a practitioner, who draws out the practical implications of the academic research. Topics will include physical and sexual violence; psychological, emotional, and economic abuse; stalking; trafficking; and childhood maltreatment, and will incorporate a gendered, feminist, or womanist analysis. Books in the series are addressed to an audience of academics and students, as well as to practitioners and policymakers.

Hilary Botein and Andrea Hetling, *Home Safe Home:*
Housing Solutions for Survivors of Intimate Partner Violence

Preventing Child Maltreatment miniseries:

Milton A. Fuentes, Rachel R. Singer, and
Renee L. DeBoard-Lucas, *Preventing Child Maltreatment*
in the U.S.: Multicultural Considerations

Esther J. Calzada, Monica Faulkner, Catherine A. LaBrenz,
and Milton A. Fuentes, *Preventing Child Maltreatment*
in the U.S.: The Latinx Community Perspective

Melissa Phillips, Shavonne Moore-Lobban, and
Milton A. Fuentes, *Preventing Child Maltreatment*
in the U.S.: The Black Community Perspective

Royleen J. Ross, Julii M. Green, and Milton A. Fuentes,
Preventing Child Maltreatment in the U.S.: American Indian
and Alaska Native Perspectives

Preventing Child
Maltreatment in the U.S.

American Indian and
Alaska Native Perspectives

ROYLEEN J. ROSS, JULII M. GREEN,
AND MILTON A. FUENTES

Rutgers University Press

New Brunswick, Camden, and Newark, New Jersey, and London

Library of Congress Cataloging-in-Publication Data

Names: Ross, Royleen (Royleen Joan), 1966- author. | Green, Julii Monette,
1976- author. | Fuentes, Milton A., author.
Title: Preventing child maltreatment in the U.S.: the American Indian and
Alaska Native perspectives / Royleen J. Ross, Julii M. Green, Milton A.
Fuentes.
Description: New Brunswick, NJ : Rutgers University Press, [2022] |
Series: Violence against women and children | Includes bibliographical
references and index.
Identifiers: LCCN 2021055692 | ISBN 9781978821101 (paperback) |
ISBN 9781978821118 (hardback) | ISBN 9781978821125 (epub) |
ISBN 9781978821132 (mobi) | ISBN 9781978821149 (pdf)
Subjects: LCSH: Child abuse—United States. | Child abuse—United
States—Prevention. | Child welfare—United States. | Indian
children—Social conditions. | Indians of North America—Social
conditions. | Alaska Native children—Social conditions. | Alaska
Natives—Social conditions.
Classification: LCC HV6626.52 .R673 2022 | DDC 362.760973—dc23
/eng/20220214
LC record available at https://lccn.loc.gov/2021055692

A British Cataloging-in-Publication record for this book is available from the
British Library.

References to internet websites (URLs) were accurate at the time of writing.
Neither the author nor Rutgers University Press is responsible for URLs that may
have expired or changed since the manuscript was prepared.

♾ The paper used in this publication meets the requirements of the American
National Standard for Information Sciences—Permanence of Paper for
Publications and Documents in Libraries and Archives, ANSI Z39.48-1992.

www.rutgersuniversitypress.org

Manufactured in the United States of America

For my children, Amanda Royce Josanaraae Cheromiah and Maredyth Benjamine Raynelle Cheromiah-Salazar; for my courageous ancestors and elders; honorable tribal leaders; tribal communities; and Our children. Extending much appreciation to Governor Perry M. Martinez for his support, prayers, and optimism.

Royleen J. Ross

For my elders, GC, IH, EC, TS, ER, MP, JP, JS & WS; for my children, STG & DAG; and for my family and the many clients who have allowed me to share in their brave journeys.

Julii M. Green

For my parents, siblings, mentors, friends, students, and clients, who have helped me learn and grow. I remain in awe of our interconnectedness.

Milton A. Fuentes

Contents

Foreword

Balance and *harmony* are two words often connoted with Indigenous feminism. Indigenous feminism values our inter-relationships with nature, between genders, across generations, and with spirit. There is harmony in respecting the gifts that each individual brings into this world. Connections are valued, and protection of our most vulnerable is prioritized. Many times, the strength, fortitude, and perseverance of Indigenous women set the tone for others. We nurture and we clearly set boundaries for safety and harmony within our group.

This book provides the reader with pertinent history through Indigenous eyes. Many of our Indian Nations were matrilineal. Women were valued as an integral part of leadership. In some traditional communities, women decided the fate of the person who assaulted them. There was a swift response to egregious behavior. Now we live by other laws. The authors examine the wounds of an imposed system of justice to help the reader better understand how to bring healing. We seek the same standards of protection under the law. We, too, want to be valued and to be heard.

Iva GreyWolf, PhD
President, Society of Indian Psychologists, 2019–2021

As Iva GreyWolf notes, throughout our histories, it has been strong Indigenous women who lead by example in our communities as they protect the most vulnerable among us. From time immemorial, our communities have loved, guided, and cherished our youngest relatives as essential for reproducing our knowledge, values, and ways of life that continue to characterize us as distinct and distinctive peoples. And yet, at present, too many of our Indigenous children are overlooked, abandoned, or even harmed by adult members of their own families. This is not to say that parents who neglect or hurt their own offspring do not care for their children; rather, for most of these parents, their own prior experiences, injuries, or impairments undermine their ability to consistently convey their love in an ideal fashion. And so, others of us must watch for instances of child maltreatment, step in to protect the most vulnerable members of our communities, and structure opportunities to intervene in appropriate and responsive ways. Somehow, some way (in too many instances), we must strive to achieve this with little help and shoestring budgets.

In consequence, maltreatment of Indigenous children creates profound predicaments for us at our intersecting identities as relatives, professionals, and tribal members. One predicament follows from a widespread Indigenous commitment to protecting and preserving the autonomy of others, leading to an ethos of social interaction frequently described as "noninterference." And yet, someone needs to interfere in episodes of child maltreatment, which themselves entail violations of personal autonomy. Indeed, as psychologists, we are professionally mandated to do so. Another predicament follows from the need to orient, educate, and mobilize powerful outsiders to help us remedy the realities of child maltreatment in our communities. And yet, sharing stories of such maltreatment threatens to reinforce the ugly stereotypes about our peoples that were created long ago to justify our dispossession and rationalize our subjugation in this nation. Indeed, we struggle today to publicly accentuate our strengths more so than our deficits, which can invite us to downplay or ignore pressing but unpleasant issues.

As you will discover in this volume, one strategy is to historicize and contextualize the legacy of Indigenous child maltreatment. One example comes from my own extended *Aaniiih*-Gros Ventre family from the Fort Belknap Indian Reservation in present-day, north-central Montana. The Gone family descends from my great-grandfather, Many-Plumes, born to Pipe-Sing and Yellow-Teeth near Chinook, Montana, in 1886. Around the age of five, he was sent to the government-run Indian industrial (boarding) school at Fort Belknap Agency. Operating under the slogan, "Kill the Indian, Save the Man," the U.S. government created such schools to deliberately assimilate Indian children into the lower echelons of American society. These schools were frequently loveless settings with rigid rules, heartless staff, and paltry funding, incubators (by default) of child maltreatment. Standard practice at these schools was to give pupils American names by adopting the father's Indian name as a surname and assigning a "Christian" name. At that time, Many-Plumes' stepfather was Gone-To-War; hence, he became Frederick Peter Gone. Fred Gone was a student at the government boarding school for ten years. According to my grandmother, Bertha (Gone) Snow, he never returned home during this entire decade, "not one time." When he emerged in 1901, he learned that his immediate family were all dead, including his own mother. No one had bothered to inform him. Grandma also explained that he spoke little about his school days: "I don't think [former students] ever really discussed it. . . . No. Because it was a real traumatic ordeal." In other words, he suffered maltreatment at school, which explained why he "hated the United States government. He hated boarding school. He would rather see [his own children] dead than go to a boarding school." Grandma elaborated: "That's why my dad wouldn't put us in a boarding school. Never would. We were the only kids that never went to boarding school [from our settlement]. The Gones. He just flat out refused to put us in boarding school. They didn't have no 'day' schools, but they had to make day schools and let us go to day school because my dad wouldn't put us there." And so, while the details of his agonies in school remain a family mystery, Fred Gone responded by ensuring that the education of his own children would not be marked by such cruelties.

Many accounts of child maltreatment in American Indian communities can be traced to ancestral boarding school experiences. My point here is that child maltreatment frequently originates from older legacies of abuse, and the clear precedent for Indigenous communities in the USA is the longstanding violence of colonialism. This is not to minimize, excuse, or deny current child maltreatment, but rather to understand it before judging it, and to intervene in ways befitting that understanding. Such is the goal of this book, to face head-on the ugliness and horror of ongoing harm to Indigenous children, even while seeking to resolutely intervene with great sensitivity to the issues. It is concurrently to acknowledge this harm even while recalling the many strengths of Indigenous survivance, and to commit to remedy even while remembering that nearly all parents love their children even when they fail to express it. And, finally, it is to recollect the Indigenous traditions surrounding child rearing that served our communities for so many millennia and that may (if we open our hearts and minds) continue to do so for many millennia to come. I am grateful to these authors for accepting this challenging task, and I am proud to commend their work to you.

Joseph P. Gone, PhD
President, Society of Indian Psychologists, 2021–2023

Preventing Child Maltreatment in the U.S.

American Indian and Alaska Native Perspectives

Introduction

At the time of the conceptualization of this book, societies in the United States literally and figuratively were living in a different world. There was no forethought about a pandemic. Colossal protests across the nation demanding social justice had not yet occurred. This was before Indian Country experienced the fury of the COVID-19 pandemic. Trepidation surrounded the conceptualization of child maltreatment from a Native perspective then, but now the sociopolitical dynamics have shifted in that courageous conversations are imperative and warranted in order for meaningful transformation of the plight of the Native child and family.

Indigenous Feminism

Writing and developing this unique, Indigenous-focused book examining child maltreatment and its impact on Native Americans and Alaska Natives in the context of Indigenous feminism has been a challenging task. The tenets of Indigenous feminism in a multiplicity of ways are contradictory to western feminism. Deer (2019) discusses the idea of monolithic feminism (rooted within a western model) and plural feminisms, which she embraces as representative of Indigenous feminism. She imparts:

> Indeed, mainstream feminism has historically failed Native women by ignoring or marginalizing issues like sovereignty and self-determination. Moreover, despite the fact that many early white

1

American feminists were influenced by Native women, early American feminists were sometimes the instigators and supporters of horrific Federal Indian law policies, including the boarding school era and child removal. Thus, it makes sense that many indigenous women categorically reject the label of "feminist" because of its Western, colonial connotations, even while supporting Native women's rights. (Deer, 2019, p. 5)

Thus, in this aspect of Indigenous feminism, the development of this book is aligned with the first principle of sovereignty and self-determination (Deer, 2019; BigFoot & GreyWolf, 2014; Wilson, 2007). We intentionally situate this text within a strength-based perspective in an effort to counter the deficit narrative about our Native U.S. children, families, and tribal communities. Providing historical context about the experiences of colonization illuminates the lived experiences of Native families and allows for a deeper understanding of the origins of child maltreatment as conceptualized today by outside entities.

Another tenet of the Indigenous feminism framework is the reliance on wisdom shared from traditional elders, both women and men, who exemplify the Native values and beliefs handed down since time immemorial (Deer, 2019; BigFoot & GreyWolf, 2014; Wilson, 2007). We reached out to established wisdom keepers within the field of psychology, social work, law enforcement, policy, and educational revolutionaries, to highlight information about child maltreatment from Native perspectives and solutions aligned with Native communities. The interconnectedness of prayer and spirituality, a third principle of Indigenous feminism (Deer, 2019; BigFoot & GreyWolf, 2014; Wilson, 2007), was also engendered after words, sentences, paragraphs, and chapters were created. Additionally, prayer and spirituality were used for asking the ancestors to help the authors and contributors to find the right words and for them to be used in the right way.

Traditional Indigenous systems are inherently egalitarian and durable, a fourth principle of Indigenous feminism (Deer, 2019; BigFoot & GreyWolf, 2014; Wilson, 2007). Indigenous feminists are humble and solid in their roles across the lifespan, as mothers, daughters, aunties, grandmothers, sisters, spouses, and nieces. They are valued and considered equals by their male counterparts; neither hierarchies nor patriarchies exist. Native women tend to their children, look after and provide for other children whether related or not, and take in children as their own. Thus, there are no orphans in the community (Simmons, 2014) and all are cared for, across the lifespan, as witnessed in the first author's tribal community. Native women wholly contribute to the health and well-being of the overall community, ceremonially, and as equalizing advocates. It is our responsibility.

During the writing of the book, some of the content was excruciatingly difficult to write for the first author, in reflection of her maternal grandparents and her Pueblo history. In contemplating the honorable life lived by her maternal grandfather, Benjamin Lorenzo, born in 1915, three years after New Mexico became a state, through his ways of being and traditional knowledge, he triumphed over commonly held western societal and educational ideals about Native Peoples. In reflection of her ancestral Pueblo People, they endured enslavement, demonization of Pueblo traditional practices, and atrocious treatment, which led to the Pueblo Revolt of 1680. In the legacy of courage, preservation of Pueblo ways of life, and the Pueblo runners in their call to duty to notify other Pueblos who banded together to overthrow the Spanish government, the American Indian/Alaska Native (AI/AN) populations are again reuniting to rewrite Our Indigenous narratives. In composing, the legacy of Pueblo running was frequently exercised in this process of writing—for prayer, for a reconciliation of the treatment of Native Peoples, and for healing. As Pueblo People, We are constantly reminded, "Our children are Our future," thus Our legacy is in their hands.

The second author is grieving and running alongside her academic sister while upholding the legacy of her Eastern Band Cherokee heritage and other Native American ancestry that was intentionally erased from her family's history. Her family members barely know their African lineage due to the enslavement of their ancestors. Additional systemic oppression contributed to secrets kept about their ties to Native communities because of the stigma attached to interracial relationships (e.g., Black and Native couples). The second author engaged in re-traditionalism to embrace customs, traditions, and values aligned with her ancestors. She stands on the shoulders of sharecroppers, caregivers, landowners, preachers, teachers, Black Nationalists, and advocates who strived for liberation.

Our Indigenous elders had no voice in the systemic, institutional, and government transgressions committed upon them, nor were they listened to when racism, oppression, and violence were used against them. Thus, in very minute ways, the content of this book is giving voice to the proverbial silenced—all of those Native children who have become Our elders and ancestors, who first-handedly suffered child maltreatment by the systems that were supposed to protect them, and the consequential outcomes. With deference, We, as Indigenous People, know the value of Our children. Reclaiming Our children interrelates with systemic, institutional, and government reformation and the rewriting of our own narrative, which is a living iterative process for western literature, western research, and western science.

Book Structure

Understanding American Indian/Alaska Native Families from the Precolonial and Contemporary Context

The first chapter of this book focuses on pre-colonization experiences of AI/AN children and families. We focus on broad discussions about AI/ANs from various regions of the United States. The authors highlight Native parenting practices, which are not typical discipline approaches based on western ideals. Native parenting practices are culturally bound strategies that seek to guide and support children. Some strategies include using humor and storytelling to evoke change or direction. Examples of tribal values from the Midwest, Plains, Southwest, Southeast, and Alaska are provided within this chapter. To understand the development of child maltreatment among AI/AN communities, we connect child maltreatment to the foster care system. The chapter concludes with a vignette of a Native child born in the modern world with current circumstances.

Systemic, Institutional, and Historical Implications of Child Maltreatment

The second chapter broadens the discussion of the influences of colonialism and systemic racism on the development of child maltreatment among AI/ANs. An overview of the U.S. educational system's impact on AI/ANs experiences takes place historically and contemporarily. The boarding school and missionary system of assimilation is addressed within this chapter. Tribal leaders were informed all children were to be formally educated and that boarding schools would be the avenue for obtaining the education. Thus, the boarding school method of removing the AI/AN child was implemented in the late 1800s. Another way the U.S. government aimed to control AI/ANs was through outlawing traditional Native religious practice. Similar to boarding schools, in missionary schools, AI/AN children experienced physical, psychological, sexual abuse, and child maltreatment though the loss of their languages, their tribal customs and beliefs, and returned home as strangers to their parents, clans, and tribal communities. The fallout from the historical trauma of the boarding school and missionary systems is what mental health professionals must contend with in the modern world.

Protective and Risk Factors

The third chapter emphasizes the importance of examining protective and risk factors that impact the well-being of AI/AN children. The authors illuminate culturally bound protective factors, including family support, ceremony, cultural revitalization (connecting to traditional ways of knowing), and mentorship. The authors also discuss the intersection of child maltreatment and risks for mental health as well as maladaptive coping strategies (e.g. substance use/dependency, suicide/suicide ideation). Adverse child experiences, contextualized through an Indigenous lens, are covered as well.

Current Policies and Laws Impacting Native Children, Adolescents, and Women

In the fourth chapter, the authors expand the discussion of AI/AN child maltreatment and the safety and protection of children, adolescents, and women. Areas include specific U.S. policies and laws related to Missing and Murdered Women and Girls, AMBER Alerts in Indian Country, medical systems, and the Indian Child Welfare Act. Restorative justice models within tribal communities are addressed in lieu of punitive measures. Specific implications for state laws and the limitations surrounding the application of federal laws that states do not adhere to or support are also explored.

Child Maltreatment Best Practices: Implications for Native Children

The fifth chapter provides an overview of the literature on culturally relevant programs and reviews government-funded programs addressing best practices through prevention, intervention, and treatment approaches that have been adapted for AI/ANs impacted by child maltreatment. The authors present an overview of programs focused on the prevention of Native child maltreatment. An overview of Native adapted treatment programs, including trauma informed care that addresses specific aspects of child maltreatment and abuse, is discussed. The chapter explores AI/AN children's mental health and the challenges to treatment.

Contemporary Cultural and Ethical Issues in Child Maltreatment

In the sixth chapter, we showcase contemporary issues involving AI/AN child maltreatment. The chapter includes an overview of the indigenist stress-coping model (Walters et al., 2002), a more applicable model for AI/AN communities addressing the socio-historical experiences of the client and discusses how it can be adapted and applied to child maltreatment. The chapter discusses ongoing relevant advocacy and intervention strategies, as well as efforts to reform child welfare. We also emphasize the intersection of environmental injustices and human exploitation in conjunction with a discussion about how the poverty and colonialism that underly these experiences impact Native children, and showcase notable incidents of sexual abuse survivors. Finally, we discuss intervention strategies and treatment planning that integrate traditional and western approaches of treatment.

Bringing It All Together: Not about Us without Us

The final chapter wraps up the book and focuses on the future directions of addressing child maltreatment in the context of AI/AN children's experiences. A three-pronged approach to next steps discusses directions for research, practice, and building community awareness as well as public support through advocacy. Included in this chapter are four suggestions for the aforementioned areas.

Summary

The writing style of this book may create curiosity for the reader, but it is written in a culturally congruent way. Mainstream and western academic literature have consistently rejected the voice of Native Peoples and authors, however, in part, this may be attributed to a different worldview and approach to conceptualization of constructs. Generally, Native languages are descriptive, thus do not reflect the same grammatical rules and structure of mainstream language in written form. Take for example the concept of religion. Many tribal nations do not have a specific word for religion, yet one of Our core values is spirituality. Worldview is also discussed in the text of the book and will elucidate differences in conceptualization of concepts, thus understanding variations in perceptions of the world through a Native lens will be an important factor in intellectualizing this book. Lyons (2000) also discusses the concept of "Rhetorical Sovereignty" for further review.

Flexibility toward the material is important when navigating the content of this text. The intent of recontextualizing and reconceptualizing child maltreatment through an Indigenous lens is to broaden the scope and understanding of child maltreatment and its implications for the AI/AN population. The wisdom keepers entrusted us with their narratives and diligently worked with us to honor their legacies.

1

Understanding American Indian and Alaska Native Families from the Precolonial and Contemporary Context

At one point, if you drew a circle, the medicine people were Aboriginal, the medicine was Aboriginal, nurses, teachers were Aboriginal. But as colonization evolved and you looked at the circle, there were no Aboriginals.

—Chief Robert Joseph

In consideration of contextualizing the history of the United States Indigenous Nations, there is no comprehensive, verifiable, and mutually agreed upon documentation of Native American history. The majority of tribes had no written language; thus, Our histories were kept through the oral tradition, which we realize often produces variable perceptions of Our past(s). With that said, the portrayal the authors present coalesces some general concepts and remembrances as articulated by a collection of respected elder Native scholars and traditional men and women who are recognized as credible resources. In addition, we rely heavily on Native scholarly books, articles, and manuscripts to maintain the authenticity of Our voices, historically and contemporarily. These purposeful efforts seek to gather and articulate a general understanding of how American Indian/Alaska Native children were raised, the roles of women, and how those intersections counter violence and historical trauma.

Collectivistic Cultural Orientation

Traditional American Indian and Alaska Native (AI/AN) family structures are generally extended-family-based and collectivistic in orientation. According to Dr. D. Subia Bigfoot, AI/AN "families come from traditionally honor based and respectful societies" (personal communication, April 5, 2018). Romero-Little et al. (2014), referring to a southwest Indigenous population, stated, "Collectivistic values are manifested in cultural constructs and in cultural approaches to socializing their children" (p. 164). Etok, an Alaska Native (AN), simply stated, "We have an inner confidence. . . . It is due to our close family ties and community life" (Gallagher, 2001, p. 39). In speaking about Native students, Pewewardy (2002) observed that AI/AN students endorse specific cultural principles including but not limited to the following: strong tribal society hierarchy, reticence, conformity to authority and respect for elders, patrimonial, matrilineal clans, and an emphasis on learning that is embedded in the teachings of the elders. In addition, Gregory Cajete, a Native science educator, reported in 1994 that geographical areas are fundamental to AI/AN identity and knowledge-based systems and are entrenched in reciprocal relationships within their surrounding environments (Cajete, 2016). Swisher and Tippeconnic (1999) found that Native people tend to have a holistic worldview where the intertwined parts of relationships are important to understanding the whole. These narratives from Indigenous tribal members and scholars encapsulate the Native way of life and illuminate the traditional support system, which continues to perpetuate Our existence in this ever-changing world.

Traditional Parenting, Child-Rearing, and Relationality

Parenting

Generally, the traditional upbringing of a child was distributed amongst members of the extended family and the community, which transcends into the contemporary family structure. Traditionally, raising a Native child in a nuclear family paradigm was a rarity. Patience, kindness, praise, respect, and humility remain the principal tenets of traditional Native parenting (National Indian Child Welfare Association [NICWA], 2016), within the context of a collectivistic orientation, as well as holistic spiritual influence and guidance.

If a child was observed to exhibit behavior outside of accepted social norms (e.g., disrespectful behavior or wrongdoing), elders and members of the community reprimanded the child without retribution from the parent, family, or clan. In fact, it was considered negligence not to correct the child and "child supervision was everyone's job. . . . The community acted as parent" (NICWA, 2016, p. 87). It was a common practice that if a child was observed to misbehave in a public tribal setting, the child was reprimanded twice, once by a community member at the time of the misdeed, then further reprimanded at home by a guardian (Jiron, 2016; R. Pecos, personal communication, September 30, 2020). While the community clearly established rules for acceptable behavior, defining expectations, and social norms, self-control was also important. "Through well-defined customs, values, and practices, which were handed down from generation to generation, parents and other care-takers, nurtured, protected, and guided children. . . . Each tribe had very positive values about children that helped keep the group strong" (NICWA, 2016, p. 86). These collectivistic approaches to raising a child provided a natural, built-in system for child protection and sustained the community over the lifespan of Native Peoples.

Relational Interconnectedness

The following are AI/AN parenting practices explained through stories from a few tribal communities. From a tribal community within the upper Midwest, Dr. D. Subia Bigfoot (personal communication, April 4, 2018) shared, "Individuals call people by their relationship (e.g., neighbor, auntie, brother, etc.), not by one's name, as a sign of respect. . . . Demonstrating a connection to a relative, we (AI/AN) are always related to someone." In the southwest, the youth commonly address members of the community as "Uncle" or "Auntie," whether related or not (Naranjo, 2017), and it was the elder's responsibility to instruct and advise the younger generation (Sakiestewa Gilbert, 2018). In many Northwest tribes, extended family relations, such as aunts and uncles, were to be addressed as parents, thus everyone shared the responsibility of raising the child (NICWA, 2016). These fundamental concepts of relatedness helped with identity development, community accountability, and protection, as not all members considered family were related by consanguinity. According to Dr. J. D. McDonald, the Lakota People, generally located in the Plains region, express "Mitákuye Oyás'iŋ" to denote an interconnectedness worldview, translating to "All my relatives," or "We are all related," or "All my relations," which further conveys the importance of relations (personal communication, July 31, 2020). This practice of identifying oneself through relationships today continues to sustain the tribal community.

Midwest Tribal Communities. In an upper Midwest tribal community, Dr. I. GreyWolf (personal communication, February 6, 2019), shared that her parents did the best that they could, given the circumstances, as both her grandmothers raised nine children during the Depression era and both grandmothers grew up in boarding schools. She further reported she and her relatives were fortunate to be guided by her grandmothers' teachings and the traditional ways of her adoptive mother (refer to chapter 3 for discussion on relationships). Dr. GreyWolf emphasized the importance of humor as a survival mechanism, remarking that finding time to laugh while enduring challenges can be healing.

Dr. GreyWolf shared her maternal grandmother was a generous spirit, always offering everyone who visited something. From sharing "corn mush to a roast" there was a sense of communal sharing. Food was also shared equally, "meaning if steak was served to the adults, it was also for the children" (personal communication, January 18, 2021). Dr. GreyWolf stated, "Treating everyone with respect, even when someone had TB, we shook hands, shared food, and our home." She further elaborated, "We had healthy boundaries and modesty within close quarters" (personal communication, February 6, 2019). Dr. GreyWolf explained how her grandmother was raised on a reservation and went to the Fort Shaw Indian School, which was a military style boarding school. She also conveyed the community took care of the needs of its members. Understandably, this included the needs of children within tribal communities.

Plains Tribal Communities. Dr. J. D. McDonald grew up between two reservations, primarily on the northern Cheyenne reservation, but was enrolled Oglala Lakota from Pine Ridge, South Dakota, where he often went back and visited relatives (personal communication, April 2, 2021). He said, "The Sioux and Cheyenne have been allies for many generations, no more clearly and dramatically than during Little Big Horn. I was so fortunate to grow up hearing stories of not only that event, but so much of what life was like during 'the old days'" (personal communication, April 2, 2021).

Dr. McDonald learned in his youth American Indian history was not recorded in western history books. His knowledge was gained from "many of the Sioux and Cheyenne elders that had either lived out, or were only two or three generations removed from the true 'old days,'" (personal communication, April 2, 2021) including the historic battle of Little Big Horn in South Dakota. He emphasized any form of violence was not traditionally ignored or rationalized, and was "*not accepted at all* under any circumstances. . . . In the old days bringing shame to one's family, clan, or tribe was unthinkable" (personal communication, April 2, 2021).

Upper Midwest Region. In the northern Plains tribal regions, "Children were so valued" and were to be indulged (J. Gone, personal communication, August 11, 2019). Dr. Joseph Gone discussed the "dearly beloved child," the child who was doted on and adored, and he related that in some instances, it was customary for siblings of this child to be sent to live with other families. Dr. Gone also intimated there were circumstances where sacred pipes were considered a "pipe child" and reverence was paid to that child (personal communication, August 11, 2019) (for additional context and extended understanding review Flannery, 1941, 1953). The idea was the pipe would get jealous. Dr. Gone stated it was a belief among the Northern Cheyenne that a child was not a full person until the child had speech, which was when they became able to access power from spirit patrons (personal communication, August 11, 2019) (for further understanding of the pipe child among the Northern Cheyenne review Straus, 1977).

He also indicated the modality of learning by the child was through listening and observing rather than through interactive, didactic instruction (personal communication, August 11, 2019) (for a thorough understanding of the Northern Cheyenne review Anderson, 2001 and Straus, 1977).

Alaska Native Traditions. In a region in Alaska, Native children were taught from a very early age about the cultural traditions, spiritual beliefs, and customs of their people, which shaped a person along with the "environment: the tundra, the river, and the Bering Sea" (Napoleon, 1996, p. 4). A well-known AN statesman, Iġġiaġruk, a.k.a. William Hensley, (2009), asserted that over five hundred generations of knowledge had passed through his people, and AN people had mastered their environment, "There is value and worth in our people" (p. 215). Proper behavior, relationships, and all things were governed "by the way of the human being, Yuuyaraq" (Napoleon, 1996, p. 4). In addition, Etok, a.k.a. Charles Edwardsen, Jr., (Gallagher, 2001) noted:

> Eskimo society is the bowhead whale and what they do with it (p. 31). . . . When you take a look at the whaling infrastructure of the Eskimo community, you must admit that we have the highest sophistication. For the Eskimos to have developed economic, moral, and social institutions based on the achievement of killing the largest mammal on earth is ingenious. (p. 253)

These doctrines, introduced early in an Alaska Native child's life were reverberated threads upheld during one's lifetime and practiced throughout the stages of development, though practiced in different maturational contexts.

Southeast Tribal Community. In a tribal community located in the Southeast, Dr. B.J.M. Brayboy shared about the value of his relationship with his extended family, and the times his maternal grandmother lived with his family, "like many Native folks did in terms of having three generations in the house" (personal communication, March 10, 2021). He discussed the intergenerational reliance they had on each other in a multiplicity of situations including working on the tobacco farm, which has remained in the family. Part of what they learned was they "were in it together" (personal communication, March 10, 2021). Dr. Brayboy was raised in a military family, thus they returned "home" after the school year ended. However, his parents were with the family "the entire time, and so who we were as Lumbee Peoples [was] always front and center in terms of what was happening in our home" (personal communication, March 10, 2021). Brayboy (2020) stated, "Indigenous peoples are grounded in the relationship between land and people that travel with them no matter where they go" (p. 26). This philosophy has shaped his perspectives and informs the critical work in which he engages.

Teachings from the Southwest. Mr. R. Pecos, former New Mexico Director of Legislative Affairs House Majority Office and Chief of Staff to House of Representatives Majority Floor Leader, shared that as he was growing up as part of a tribal population in the Southwest, he had been gifted the "opportunity to learn to love (his) language, culture, people, and community" (personal communication, September 30, 2020). When gifted those experiences, he asked himself how one could not do everything in one's life to reciprocate and bestow those gifts to others. Mr. Pecos imparted he felt this love was "the heart of who we ultimately become . . . , a driving force in everything I have tried to do and being very conscious of my grandfather's teaching about giving value to everything that defines who we are; language especially and cultural knowledge" (personal communication, September 30, 2020).

Another traditionalist and an organizational executive director in the Southwest, Mr. G. Vigil, eloquently articulated that the foundational basis for an overarching exceptional quality of life is found in "living your creation story" (personal communication, May 22, 2019). Mr. Vigil further iterated this aspect of a traditional upbringing was entwined with "living spiritually with the wisdom of the elders, in connection with a higher power," stressing that because it is an ingrained way of life, one does not think about this concept often (personal communication, May 22, 2019). Regarding this Southwest population, Sando (1992) imparts "there were guidelines for well-ordered living" (p. 25) that were given to The People by the Great One. The structure of the extended family and the spiritual doctrines of a traditional way of life are the foundations of a fulfilled existence. Sando also expounded on the social structure of this population, with nonexistent crime and fear, which will be discussed in subsequent chapters.

Givers of Life. Dr. D. Subia Bigfoot (personal communication, April 4, 2018) reported in a tribal community represented in the central Midwest, a pregnant woman giving birth does not make a sound as she practices relaxation techniques and sets an intention of peace for the birth of her child. Delivery was not meant for being overwhelmed; essentially, the mother did not want the baby to think it was causing her pain. Women are the givers of life, absorbing and passing on pain in a different way, more devoted to the children in that way. This concept also applies to the timing of birthing children. In some tribes, such as in Alaska, depending upon the seasonal conditions, women were instructed about the timing of a pregnancy, and if the impending conditions were read as harsh or severe, women were counseled the timing of a pregnancy may not be warranted due to the anticipated hardship (Kawagley, 2006). Dr. Rita Pitka Blumenstein, the first certified Alaska Native tribal doctor recognized in Alaska, iterated a child's first knowledge was obtained during pregnancy and the healthy development of the baby must occur in a peaceful environment with both parents (Kemberling & Avellaneda-Cruz, 2013). In Southwest populations, there are "Native-based ontological understandings of newborns, and their abilities are framed by the mother tongue. It is this epistemology of human existence that guides (parents') sacred responsibility for the care of infants and young children" (Romero-Little, 2011, p. 92). And this contributes to the socialization process and "cultural plans" Native parents have for their children.

In the central Midwest, some tribes aspire to the Seven Gifts of the Grandfathers, imparting lessons for life, which include love, respect, honesty, bravery, humility, truth, and wisdom. These gifts are introduced in the very early stages of a child's life and serve to guide a person's life. In general, the Alaska Native Department of Health and Human Services (DHHS) Commissioner Valerie Nurr'araaluk Davidson stated, "Concepts of nature and nurture were understood intrinsically. Even the words or mannerisms of the expectant mother and those around her were understood to affect the unborn child" (p. 7). Also, in some Northwest tribes, shortly after a child was born, female members of the community would gather, praising the baby, and would often make oratory declarations about the child's future (NICWA, 2016).

Identity Foundations

These recounted parenting practices remain the foundations of Native existence in an ever-changing, challenging world. "A general underlying belief was that children were as much a part of the group as everyone else and should be respected" (NICWA, 2007, p. 86). Native children were raised in a dignified environment and their voices were heard. The modality of learning was listening and less about didactic instruction (J. Gone, personal communication, August 11, 2019). Prior to European contact, the tribes of North America existed with intact community self-awareness and purpose that entailed complete educational systems for raising their children (Tafoya & Del Vecchio, 2005). Though one may assert the aforementioned information presented romanticizes tribal existence or that a Utopian existence is portrayed in the accounts of the tribal members, the way of life of tribal Peoples subsisted and flourished for thousands of years, guided by these many tenets, without the intervention of any other societal influences and impositions.

Each tribe lived in relative isolation from other Indigenous people and identification was accomplished "by our own traditional tribal affiliations assigned by our Creator" (Ross, 2018, p. 4). Weaver (2001) stated, "Before contact, indigenous people identified themselves as distinct from other indigenous people and constructed their identities in this way" (p. 242). The names associated with tribes today are manifestations of outsiders' nomenclature and taxonomy. However, some tribes have returned to their original identification designations. For example, in 1986, the Tohono O'odham Nation in Arizona successfully returned to identification of themselves by their own name.

Culture and Gender Roles; Identity and Cultural Preservation

Although each tribal community used specific cultural and linguistic methods to educate their children, tribes had rules about distinct skills that had to be gained before a youth was accepted as an adult member of the tribe, sometimes acknowledged in the community by rites-of-passage ceremonies (NICWA, 2016). The system facilitated the transmission of cultural values, Indigenous languages, and practices. The child's special skills, proclivities, and temperament might influence their role within the tribe (Tafoya & Del Vecchio, 2005). Each child was expected to be aware and competent in all three areas. For example, a male youth who was exceptionally skilled in subsistence abilities (e.g., prosperous hunter, fisherman, agriculturalist) would spend more time engaged in supplying food for the tribe, or being a maker of drums or moccasins, which were significant responsibilities. Or a female youth who might be adept at basket weaving, pottery making, or traditional sewing (e.g., buckskin, seal skins, etc.) would be nurtured in her abilities. Contemporarily, according to Naranjo (2017), "Still today one can still see children in the community being given tasks that in another society would seem inappropriate for a child" (p. 25). Specific roles and responsibilities were delineated for members of the tribe. Spiritual rituals were conducted in order to facilitate large hunts and harvests with participation by all members of the community, including children.

There is an intersection of the abovementioned competencies that contribute to the core of individual Native identities, and Indigenous communities, within a collectivistic society. Naming ceremonies established the child's identity in the tribe (NICWA, 2016) and in the spirit world. The name bestowed upon a Native child had significance in that the name was reassigned from an ancestor; the name resembled an event or object of importance gifted by Mother Earth; or the name was derived from an event of magnitude the child undertook. "A child's traditional name creates stronger familial connections between the naming member of the community, but can also transcend the barrier of time to create linear relational paths between ancestors, introduce children to the spirits of nature, and/or teach mindfulness of the life defining events" (M. Cheromiah, personal communication, March 19, 2019).

The child's name could also change due to maturation. The naming of a child was substantial in a Native child's persona (Romero-Little, 2011) and within some tribes, demarcated with a feast or gathering of family and community at the time of the ceremony. A study conducted by Ross (2018) in a Southwest population, with 330 participants, yielded results indicating the proclivity to give Indian names remained of paramount importance in the Native population in contemporary times. In fact, within some Native communities, many individuals are only known to others by their Indian name and their anglicized names remain a community mystery.

The overall welfare of tribal members, including children, was principal to a tribal community. There was a balance in allowing a child to explore their environment with curiosity and in maintaining boundaries for safety. Regarding discipline, it "was never separated from teaching the right way to do things" (NICWA, 2016, p. 206), which was closely associated with spiritual beliefs. In some tribes, the physical representation of an individual or an entity representing a disciplinary figure was used as a means to mediate a child's behavior, which remains protected tribal knowledge. Some tribes used teasing as a way to address a misdeed. After the child learned from their error, the teasing ceased and the behavior changed (Garrett & Garrett, 1994; NICWA, 2016). Another form of discipline included temporarily shunning a child, which might employ the entire family not speaking to the child or the parent not acknowledging the child for a brief period of time, which gave the child the opportunity to reflect on the transgression (NICWA, 2016). These methods are still used today to correct behavior that is not conducive to the family or community. Physical punishment was nonexistent and "moral development received constant and careful attention" (NICWA, 2016, p. 99) which are also parenting practices used today, however circumstances extensively discussed in chapter 2 have changed the family unit dynamics.

Native Humor

Within the context of the tribal community, humor is used as an effective method of mitigating all types of social situations. Native humor is used to create and maintain relations for generations in many forms (Garrett & Garrett, 1994). Children are introduced to this construct early in their infancy and, similar to a faithful companion, humor remains a part of the person for the duration of their life. In some tribes, teasing is intergenerational, as early in a child's life, grandparents tease an infant about their ability to cook or hunt and the other grandparent will playfully take the grandchild's side and defend them. In addition, Native humor can have components of healing rifts, tempering situations, and teaching humility. Sometimes a very serious child will be teased in different ways so they have a lighter approach to the world around them.

As a Native scholar and published author, Vine Deloria Jr.'s discussion about Native humor in his 1969 book *Custer Died for Your Sins* was iconic and groundbreaking in that era. He introduced the strategy of humor in politics, various relationships, and having to provide explanations to outsiders in order to understand the pun. Garrett et al. (2005) stated, "Native humor as a spiritual tradition often goes unnoticed by people from the mainstream culture as a powerful healing force in the lives of Native people, as it has been for ages" (p. 195). Unto itself, humor is a powerful manner of communication for Indigenous Peoples. Consider the following:

> Humor has served as one of the many useful coping methods for generations of Native people who have learned how to survive in the face of persecution, exploitation, and genocide.... The use of humor in Native tradition has contributed to the survival of many Native nations as a coping skill, to maintaining harmony and a balance among Native people as an everyday communication skill that preserves connections, and to the life-learning of younger generations as an oral tradition that shows people how to live or how not to live. (Garrett et al., 2005, p. 202)

All My Relations

Traditional Law

A misconception exists that before contact, what is now considered "law and order" was non-existent in tribal communities and anarchy was rampant. In fact, tribes had very sophisticated systems of governance as Kawagley (2006) exemplifies in his discussion of the elaborate Yupiaq traditional code of conduct. The elders orally emphasized the laws to members of the community, and because theirs were not written laws, the Yupiaq were misconstrued as lawless. However, within a collectivistic orientation, social interactions and harmonious relationships are paramount within the community. In part, this social harmony is attributed to survival of the overall collectivistic group. From minor to severe infractions, traditional law mitigated and negotiated internal conflicts and relationships. Edmo stated,

"There was a strong social responsibility in a tribe and everyone had to get along and the common goal was to have a good life for all" (NICWA, 2016, p. 206). The way to navigate relationships in various circumstances was modeled to children and social justice was mandated to maintain social order.

One of the most severe punishments was banishment from the tribe. Thus, the family or clan had a significant responsibility in maintaining social welfare (Deloria & Lytle, 1983). As a result, within Indigenous tribal family, community, and kinship structures, conflict was minimal to avoid bringing disrespect or embarrassment upon the family or clan members "as their means of determining the proper social response and penalty for violation of the tribal customs" (Deloria & Lytle, 1983, p. 82). Currently, as a means of consequence for egregious behavior, tribes continue to utilize banishment as a last resort, a sovereign right, with tribal members for various severe infractions, without the individual being stripped of tribal membership status in some cases (Kunesh, 2007). Generally, restorative justice is accomplished through the individual not being allowed back into the tribal homelands and/or not authorized to participate in activities for a period of time. The individual might also make restitution through behavior changes, and once the atonement period concludes, the individual is allowed to return back to full status as a member of the community. Restorative justice in tribal communities is resurging in some tribes as a traditional approach to resolving conflict and for restoring order in a more harmonious way (refer to chapter 4 for more referenced information).

Space and Place

In historical and contemporary times, two essential doctrines in the upbringing of an Indigenous child pertain to the acknowledgement of ancestors—their presence, influence, and relationship with the surrounding environment, and secondly, forging socioecological relationships. These socioenvironmental relationships also have implications in religious practices, ancestral residential and burial sites, subsistence activities, and lifeways (Preucel & Pecos, 2015). All of these aspects of a Native child's nurturing are routinely discounted by dominant society, psychological and medical professionals, and in educational realms; however, these facets remain important aspects of many Indigenous children's lives and identity. Appreciating and honoring who We are and where We come from cements our foundations for who We are today and who We are to become. "Indian children were taught to observe their natural surroundings and learn from what they saw. They were taught that all of nature was a teacher and an ally" (NICWA, 2016, p. 232).

Dr. Joseph Gone documented the importance of space and place from an Indigenous worldview in his article, "'So I Can Be Like a Whiteman': The Cultural Psychology of Space and Place in American Indian Mental Health." Dr. Gone asserts interpersonal relatedness to the environment and relationality in "participation in indigenous ritual spaces enacted or performed in designated sacred places on or near the reservation" is important (2008, p. 392), and differs from mere admiration of a landscape or occupation of a prized land space. The concept of relationality to land (Brayboy & Chin, 2020; Isaacs et al., 2018) is relevant today as an attribute of many Indigenous children's lives and their relation to their environment and the world (refer to chapter 3 for more on relationality and interconnectedness). However, "cultural appropriation and our history have taught us to be protective and secretive about our beliefs and ceremonies" (GreyWolf, 2018, para. 5). Thus, we hold our most sacred beliefs, thoughts, and values to ourselves, within our societies and communities, as a protective factor and in fortification of the continuity of our traditional teachings.

Generosity of Spirit

"Giving Back"

One of the essential tenets emphasized within Indigenous culture is the western concept of philanthropy or altruism. Simply defined, these are practices associated with "giving back" to the community, an interwoven gift and responsibility. Many Indigenous Peoples believe that this social responsibility exceeds philanthropic or altruistic meanings. Romero (1994) imparts, "The inclusive view that each individual, from the time of birth, is a vital element of community, encourages the nurturing of individual strengths and the pursuit of personal interests in relation to others through the promotion of positive contribution or 'giving back' to one's community" (p. 52).

"Giving back" permeates each member of the collectivistic community and has obligatory rites associated within the social structure of the tribe. The contributions are correlated with age and skill, as all members of the collectivistic society participate. "Giving back" is a lifetime endeavor and encompasses responsibility by all. This effort, practiced over the lifespan, may be represented in traditional and/or contemporary ways, such as participation in ceremony, song, dance, or via professional career knowledge one has acquired. Often, an individual's community responsibility of "giving back" encompasses all the roles and forums in which one is charged as a tribal member.

Traditional "Pay It Forward"

From the collectivistic perspective of many tribal members, sharing connotes a repeated giving without expectation of return or keeping tabulation. As asked by an anonymous Native educator, "Have any of you thought about the concept of 'saving' as in for 'retirement?'" This thought baffled this Native person, as they knew they could go back to their reservation, could live very inexpensively, and barter their skills. This person also noted, "There was no concept of saving, as one knew there would always be more, because we shared." This concept also profoundly applies to the sharing of food. Many mothers, grand-mothers, aunties, and sisters routinely cooked meals not only for their own children and family relations, but for other children and those in need in the community. The feeding of other children brought great joy and delight to the cooks. But this was true for the menfolk as well. The first author vividly recalls her maternal grandfather, a rancher and cattleman, delivering a lamb or sheep to families that he observed struggling, without any expectation of repayment. These concepts were heavily emphasized and modeled daily to children during their upbringing.

Contemporary Considerations

Language

In contemporary times, some tribes continue to teach their Indige-nous languages as a first language to their infants, toddlers, and children. Many traditional Native languages have implications for a Native person's overall being, as the language itself has life. Astonish-ingly, a school in the southwest exists, erected in 2014 (Preucel & Pecos, 2015), wherein Native children up to the age of six are solely instructed in a Native language and between ages six and twelve, the educational curriculum is taught equally in the Native language and

English. Translation from traditional languages to English at times can create confusion, since there is not a one-to-one interpretation for many words or concepts; Native languages are primarily descriptive, and word meanings translate differently. For example, in the Alaska Native population, there are approximately fifty words used to describe the concept of snow. Each word is distinct and has meaningful connotations, according to an Inupiat elder.

Although today the penalties for a child speaking in their Native tongue in educational settings are not as severe as when ancestors were forced into boarding schools, reminders remain everywhere in today's world and in the dominant society that English is the only accepted language for Indigenous children. Fortunately, the Indian Self-Determination and Education Assistance Act (ISDEAA), Pub. L. 93–638, enacted in 1975, liberated Indian education and tribes began operating programs via acquired authority, contracting with the Federal government (Indian Self-Determination and Education Assistance Act, 2009). Henceforth, many tribes have erected their own school systems within their own tribal nations. In tribally run schools, Indigenous language instruction has been implemented into some curriculums and encourages traditional language use. Educational instruction in this arena, inclusive of the Arts and Sciences, is taught using tribally originated themes, creating a "linguistically and culturally rich learning environment that supports the fundamental principles and core values of native life," (Preucel & Pecos, 2015, p. 233), such as with the Keres Children's Learning Center, Indigenous Montessori Institute. The U.S. Census (2012) documented 28 percent of the Native population, age five and older, spoke a language other than English at home.

Intelligence

Regarding the constructs of intelligence or giftedness of Native children, many Native nations ascribe to the philosophy that all children are gifted in various aspects. Generally, the belief that only some Native children were bestowed with superior intelligence or unique giftedness is incongruent with a collectivistic value system. Inclusively, all Native children are thought to have intelligence and each child possesses giftedness in various ways. Romero (1994) states, "'Giftedness' is a global human quality encompassed by all individuals" (p. 41). Romero (1994) also redefines intelligence and giftedness from a Native perspective, which measures constructs that western society deem significant. In Romero's study, she demonstrated the same criteria that constituted the Full Scale IQ score (FSIQ) and abilities measured by Weschler psychological assessment instruments and Woodcock-Johnson tests (Ross, 2018).

Role Models

Modeling good behavior and providing role models for children to follow were important aspects of a child's upbringing. The bidirectional relationship between adults and children was understood, and as children patterned themselves after adept individuals, leaders acted in "a good way" as they knew children imitated them (NICWA, 2016, p. 205). The elders always say, "Children are innocent spirits and they hear and they learn and they absorb even when we think they are not" (Regis Pecos, personal communication, September 30, 2020). Thus, Native children became proficient at early ages in culturally based skills (Naranjo, 2017). The Native child both observed and was instructed in knowledge about healthy ways of living and necessary skills for living. These methods of a traditional education established the foundation of the existence of tribal societies for millenniums. Mr. G. Vigil affirmed the facets of the traditional passing of knowledge via modeling paradigms remain an important part of culture, ceremonies, and role responsibilities (personal communication, May 22, 2019).

Talking Circles

Another important aspect of Native culture relates to storytelling, song, narratives, generational stories, and dialogue. These Indigenous methodological instruments were used to teach lessons and impart knowledge to children. Further, these modes of communication were modeled to children representing healthy communication styles, inclusive of interwoven and interconnected life constructs, as ways of conveying one's thoughts. Ed Edmo related the following about Old Man Coyote, used in many Native traditional teachings:

> Old Man Coyote is the most infamous teacher of culture. Old Man Coyote doesn't have an advanced degree from any college, has never sat on a national juvenile delinquency panel, nor has Old Man Coyote been asked to give any position papers at an Indian national

conference and yet, Old Man Coyote has been a primary teacher of Indian children throughout the ages. (NICWA, 2016, p. 127)

Talking circles continue to remain a vital part of contemporary Native culture in which children also partake. These venues, convened for a multiplicity of purposes, illustrate turn taking, respect for other's perspectives, listening, and resolution. Socially acceptable behaviors are reinforced in this way.

Communitarianism Strength

Previous references to the overall well-being of a tribal member, child, adolescent, or adult, are embedded in the components of a life-style that, to dominant society, is deficient in innumerable ways. Viewed through a western Eurocentric lens, it is incredulous Native Peoples do not aspire to the tenets of meritocracy. In addition, it baffles educators, politicians, lawmakers, and agents of the government that even today Native People have not accumulated significant wealth and the continued sharing of resources is a waste. Further, the simplicity of a tribal person's lineage and family relations is constantly judged and assaulted by the dominant society, especially the family unit that consists of myriad relations. Native children are ridiculed for their definition of family and for having an abundance of parents, grandparents, and siblings. However, this is the strength and resilience which We, as Native People, carry, and with which We survive and thrive. We continue to maintain harmonious relationships with all things as best we can, despite efforts to destroy, exploit, and strip our tribal land bases and our traditional ways of being, including our traditional food sources and subsistence activities, all of which we continue to maintain relationships.

Removal

The National Congress of American Indians (2021b) reported 26.8 percent of the AI/AN population lives in poverty, based on a 2017 statistic. The Native population represents the poorest segment of American society. AI/AN families have poverty rates close to 30 percent, meaning almost three out of ten family's incomes are insufficient to meet the needs associated with a very modest standard of living (Snipp & Saraff, 2011). AI/ANs have historically been concentrated in remote, rural locations (as reservations were purposely established away from the mainstream of American society). Many reservation communities have been grounded in tribal culture as well as in the preservation of tribal sovereignty. However, they have also been the economic backwaters steeped in unemployment and poverty (Snipp & Saraff, 2011). The effects of poverty, which is one of the largest contributing factors to the status of AI/AN nations, are unfortunately all too often construed as child neglect and often fester amongst professionals who make false assumptions and egregious decisions, purportedly on behalf of Native children, based on this, and have for generations. Consider that before the Indian Child Welfare Act (ICWA) in 1978, 25–35 percent of Native children had been removed from their families, institutionalized, fostered, or adopted out, with 90 percent of those placements occurring in non-Indian homes (NICWA, 2019). Today, despite ICWA, Native children remain four times more likely than Whites to be removed and placed in foster care (NICWA, 2019). As far as government initiatives are concerned, this practice has been an effective means of cultural genocide for decades.

In summation, the needs of Native children were met historically and continue to be met in established modern U.S. society by Native parents, guardians, and caretakers. Wallis (2002) affirmed that Natives did not view themselves as lacking anything. In the psychological constructs of Maslow's Hierarchy of Needs (see Blackfoot Nation foundation), western education emphasizes that Native children are remiss in not partaking of college and university higher learning and taught they are somehow missing the upper echelon of self-actualization. However, in this conceptualization, similar to the experience of the first author, it is a difficult feat to understand and accept that Indigenous Peoples do not need to obtain a highly coveted higher education to serve their communities or other Indigenous Peoples and can be fully self-actualized with or without a higher education.

Transcending Generational Existence

In summary, all of these afore-referenced aspects are the composition of a Native child. Hundreds of years ago and today. Thousands of years ago and today. Unfortunately, due to the multitude of governmental and societal negative influences, there now exists a plethora of social and medical maladies the U.S. Indigenous population confronts daily. The status of the Native population has changed, which has understandably impacted the family unit and the Native child. The following vignette, using translated Indian names, provides an example of the contemporary circumstances and reality within which the Native family endures:

River was born in a metropolitan city, not by his Native mother's (Rain) choice, but by dictation of the systemic hospital policy that infant deliveries were no longer viable within her remote tribal lands; all mothers were required to report to the hospital at thirty-two weeks. The non-Native hospital medical staff dictated pregnant mothers had to stay in lodging accommodations near the hospital until delivery. The tribal hospital employed Rain for several years and she drove 120 miles daily round trip for work. She was in a non-essential position and was furloughed during the government shutdown. The shutdown devastated Rain and her husband, Thunder, financially. The bills piled up, as they lived paycheck to paycheck. They had received shut off notices for their lights and gas and recently had to go to the food bank for groceries to supplement items in their nearly bare pantry. Both Rain and Thunder came from big families and because they both worked, they were able to contribute to other family members' hardships, since they had been through rough times before, and their families helped to take care of them. Because of ICWA, Rain and Thunder had legal custody of their two nieces and a nephew, all between the ages of four and eight. Their parents were both deceased because of drinking contaminated water from a government supported oil drilling well located upstream from their rural home on the reservation. At the time of the government shutdown, the eight-year-old, Cloud, told his teacher that his mom and dad might get divorced because he heard them yelling at each other and they might have to move out of where they were living. Cloud said the house was cold, all the kids had to sleep on one bed, he had to watch his younger sisters because his mom and dad had to work, and he was hungry. The teacher immediately called Office of Child Services (OCS) and reported a case of child neglect.

The circumstances contained in the vignette are demonstrative of current systemic pressures a Native child and family endure daily. Although the majority of Native parents are unquestionably fit to raise their own children, an underlying apprehension exists within the family and tribal community based upon historical implications pertaining to the unconstitutional, hence unlawful, removal of Native children based upon ill conceptualized information by members of non-Native entities. Arguably, the concentrated efforts of historical systematic initiatives targeting Native children have contributed to the attempted decimation of the Native family, community, and spirituality of tribal nations.

2

Systemic, Institutional, and Historical Implications of Child Maltreatment

> Indigenous peoples occupy a liminal
> space that accounts for both the
> political and racialized natures of
> our identities (Toward a Tribal
> Critical Race Theory).
> —Bryan McKinley Jones Brayboy,
>   Lumbee, PhD (2005); ASU
>   vice president of Social
>   Advancement; senior advisor
>   to the president

Changing Perspectives

In Indian Country, conceptualization of child maltreatment necessitates a radical perspective shift from western viewpoints, theoretical models, and practices toward systemic and institutional etiology. This perspective change has implications for education, politics, the judicial system, psychology, and social welfare environments. These considerations are introduced in this chapter as a way to understand the larger systemic structures contributing to child maltreatment in the AI/AN population and are not an attempt to reassign responsibility from an emic perspective, but to establish the groundwork for an understanding from a global perspective as it pertains to the Native community. "In almost all cases there is flagrant inaccuracy of the role of the Indian in American history" (Sando, 1992, p. 142). As emphasized in the first chapter, child maltreatment was not embedded in traditional Native culture. The social structure, a collectivistic culture, maintained societal order, thus exhibiting the tenets of communitarianism (Kawagley, 2006). The introduction of the concept of abuse and heteropatriarchy came with contact by other foreign nations.

The convenient blame for the maltreatment of Native children is entrenched in the many social systems and professionals within those systems that astutely pass judgment and point fingers at Indigenous parents and communities. The challenge in reconceptualizing child maltreatment lies within the courageous conversations that must be had among members in dominant society and Native experts (e.g., Indian Country professionals, academics, tribal leaders, Indigenous elders, etc.). Honest conversations must occur for overall improvement of the current conditions of the Native child. Unfortunately, difficult dialogues have the potential to lead to defensiveness (DiAngelo, 2018) during attempts to discuss deconstructing and decolonizing child maltreatment. These discussions must include topics such as the systemic effects of racism and oppression, forced assimilation, the horrendous educational system, ineffective one-size-fits-all approaches, and stratified poverty.

Quandary of U.S. Educational Institutions

School Purpose

One central consideration of child maltreatment for the AI/AN child is found within the formal orthodox western educational setting. Historically, the government's policy on Indian education was predetermined to fail (Ross, 2018). From the late 1800s and into the 1950s, the education of Indigenous Peoples was conducted within a westernized educational structure foreign to them, without an indigenized identity space. Oka Kte, Lakota, surmised, "I could think of no reason why white people wanted Indian boys and girls except to kill them, and not having the remotest idea of what a school was, I thought we were going east to die" (Cooper, 1999, p. 1) when he referenced leaving the Great Plains in 1879. Indian education policy during this era was largely focused on the assimilation of Native children into the dominant society, usually at the hands of various church denominations or the U.S. government. This was a calculated peccadillo aimed at destroying the Native family through destroying the family structure by detaching children from their parents and culture. Consider the fact that Carlisle Indian Industrial School in Pennsylvania was erected in 1879, three years after the Battle of Little Bighorn and right before the Mankato Massacre of 1880 in Minnesota.

Also during the late 1800s, simultaneously while Native children were relinquished to institutional schools, this was a significant transitory time for the *Aaniih*-Gros Ventre. Buffalo hunts occurred wherein approximately one hundred bison were pushed over a cliff. Prior to horses, this was the old way of hunting them, for the purpose of feeding the entire tribe across the lifespan. Eventually, this practice gave way to equestrian hunting and that shifted gender roles (J. Gone, personal communication, August 10, 2019). The buffalo hides began to have economic implications for the tribe and were considered a cash economy. Dr. J. Gone imparted the tanning was left to the women, which was back-breaking work. Because mounted hunters could kill many more buffalo in a single hunt, more women's labor was needed to process all the hides into robes for the fur trade. This led to men taking many wives, which "dramatically altered gender relations and status differences between men and women" (personal communication, August 10, 2019, as first argued by Patricia Albers; for an expanded understanding of AI gender roles review Albers, 1983). These acts of war and newly minted economic implications resulted in the upset of family dynamics. Thus, a newly devised reformed act of war was crafted, targeting Native women and children, where Indigenous women's roles were no longer egalitarian (Bigfoot & GreyWolf, 2014) and Native children were a commodity for strategic play in annihilating the Native family, Native languages, Native spirituality and religious practice, and Native culture (refer to chapter 1 for further insight of how Native children were revered).

During this period, Native children were also literally stolen from tribal lands at times (Cooper, 1999) for attendance at these government sanctioned educational institutions. This resulted in a "highly sanitized refinement of a systematic, yet unspoken, cultural genocide program that existed for nearly a century" (McDonald & Chaney, 2003, p. 44). Consequently, this led to an immeasurable loss of Native cultural heritage and impairment in parenting skills in Native families. These circumstances substantially contributed to intimate partner violence and child abuse within Native families (Willis & Spicer, 2013). In addition, these circumstances likely contributed to adoption of a patriarchal mindset in Native communities, and disrupted displays of affection and restricted levels of emotionality. This "civilized" educational paradigm instigated Native children learning the tenets of institutional living and learning to be ashamed of their cultural heritage (NICWA, 2016).

AI/AN children also experienced child maltreatment through the loss of their languages, their tribal customs and beliefs, and they would return home as strangers to their parents, clans, societies, and tribal communities. AI/AN children were subject to physical, psychological, and sexual abuse within these educational systems (McDonald, et al., 2018; Tafoya & Del Vecchio, 2005). Cultural genocide was rampant. Etok, of AN origin, succinctly captured the essence of his and others' experience in a Bureau of Indian Affairs boarding school when speaking his Native language and being addressed by a non-Native educator:

> If you want to be an Indian all your life, nothing but a salmon
> cruncher, just keep on talking Indian. You can just go back to the
> village and rot for the rest of your life. But if you want to amount to
> something, if you want to grow up and hold a job as a secretary or
> laborer and make good money and live like a white man, then you
> better listen to what I am teaching you, and start speaking *English*.
> (Gallagher, 2001, p. 77)

The Native child in this situation was purposely stripped of all things Indigenous, including the intrinsic value of the interrelational aspects of their cultural, familial, socioecological, and spiritual arenas.

Native children were held hostage within various government and church-sanctioned educational institutions, with no recourse for parents to regain custody of their children. Numerous Native children sustained horrific, multiple abuses at these institutions of learning. Currently, layers of religious cover-ups are frequently unfolding in the media, chronicling decades of abuse. Churches are finally being held accountable for the multitudes of abuses levied and covered up by church officials. One tragic story related to a Native woman who endured countless sexual assaults, along with her nine sisters at a boarding school. Her account includes speculation she may have committed ghastly deeds. In her own words, she recounted the following:

"Father Francis took me to the church basement where they stored coffins when somebody died," she said. "He would lift me up and tell me that if I didn't do what he told me to, he would put me in a coffin." She said he forced her to perform oral sex on him and knows of other girls who became pregnant. "They aborted the babies right there at the school," she said, "and burned the fetuses in the incinerator. I worked in the incinerator room, and anything Sister brought down in that bucket, I just had to put it in the incinerator." She added, weeping openly: "When I look back, I wonder if I had to burn any fetuses." (Hilleary, 2018, para. 9–12)

Across the United States, there remain countless untold stories of clergy abuse of children. Many Native victims have remained silent, experiencing wide-ranging shame and guilt. This silence has manifested in substance use disorders (Pember, 2016), depression (McDonald, et al., 2018; Pember, 2016), and suicide (Pember, 2016) with etiology based in historical and contemporary complex traumas, including unresolved trauma, from these boarding school indignities.

The boarding school method of removing the AI/AN child was implemented toward the end of the 1800s (Tafoya & Del Vecchio, 2005). "The Meriam Report" of 1928 asserted tribal leaders were informed that all children were to be formally educated, and boarding schools would be the avenue for obtaining education (Meriam et al., 1928). Non-compliance meant Native parents were threatened with imprisonment as a strategy (Johnston-Goodstar & VeLure Roholt, 2017), permanent removal of their children was the price to pay, and threats of withholding of their government issued rations were used which signified starvation. As an alternative, children were rounded up and physically stolen from their tribal lands to attend these schools (Cooper, 1999).

Unfortunately, for many Native households and families, the ultimate price of education was the life of their children, many of whom died at these government and missionary-sanctioned schools (McDonald & Chaney, 2003). For example, Carlisle Indian School, operating between 1879 and 1918, documented nearly 200 burial graves for students who died at this institution established for "learning" (Carlisle Indian School Digital Resource Center, n.d.). The full accounting of Native child deaths at these institutions has either not been tallied or remains clandestine. Some students who fell ill at the school for various reasons were sent home to die so as not to blemish the school record (Cooper, 1999). These educational institutions, through harsh systematic methodologies, aimed to assimilate Native children into western culture. The impact of Native children's deaths, under the guise of education, has become woven into the contemporary fabric of Native families and contributes to intergenerational trauma for the Native population.

Experimentation. Dr. I. GreyWolf's (personal communication, February 6, 2019) grandmother went to the Fort Shaw Indian School (a military style boarding school), and she and other Native youth there were subjects of medical experimentation, including brain surgery. In fact, Dr. GreyWolf's grandmother was the only one of seven Native children experimented upon who could walk or talk after enduring brain surgery. Dr. GreyWolf noted, "I remember my grandmother shared memories about the painful surgery recovery when I asked her about a hole behind her ear. Grandma talked about there being tubes and a metal plate in her head. She remembered the painful twisting of tubes" (personal communication, February 6, 2019). It is evident the treatment that Dr. GreyWolf's grandmother and other Native children experienced while in boarding schools was in fact institutional child abuse and maltreatment. Dr. GreyWolf further conveyed that these abusive boarding school experiences perpetuated more abuse within many Native households, impacting traditional ways of parenting and parent-child relationships; "[by] systemic treatment of ancestors, the oppressor's behaviors manifested within individuals" (personal communication, February 6, 2019). The extent of experimentation, medical or otherwise, on Native children remains unknown.

Dr. GreyWolf's paternal grandfather documented his own harsh treatment at boarding school. His personal stories of the abuses he experienced are documented in an Eau Claire, Wisconsin museum. Dr. GreyWolf said, "Although there is no history of sexual abuse within my family, there is a long history of harsh corporal punishment/physical abuse as a consequence of having three of my grandparents essentially raised in boarding schools." One way to contend with poverty and the systemic injustices they experienced is through education. Dr. GreyWolf (personal communication, February 6, 2019) reported:

> Exposure to child development courses informed me about being a better parent. Additionally, I was adopted by a traditional family that reinforced traditional values, provided direction, and were a sounding board. In fact, from when my children were in pre-school, I raised my family within an alcohol-free home. Our family was also involved in ceremony, contributing to and learning the importance of traditional ways.

One must ponder the traumatic outcomes and manifestations today in contemporary conceptualization of Native child maltreatment that are implicated by, and correlated with, the impact of the type of experiences such as those had by Dr. GreyWolf's family.

For example, Dr. J. D. McDonald observes, "I knew children were being maltreated around me growing up on the Rez. Everybody knew . . . I believe people from all cultures on this earth believe child abuse and domestic violence are wrong, terribly wrong" (personal communication, April 2, 2021). He said when he started graduate school, he directly spoke to as many elders as he could to ask them about the violence in tribal communities. Dr. McDonald indicated, "They consistently pointed to such factors as forced relocation to a reservation way of life (and everything that came from that), the boarding school era, and the introduction of alcohol as the predictors of domestic violence in all its forms" (personal communication, April 2, 2021). He poignantly related that the elders invariably finished their stories, often with tears in their eyes, by shaking their head and saying things like "That's not the way it's supposed to be" or, "That's not the way we're supposed to act" (personal communication, April 2, 2021).

Contemporary School Conditions. Currently, western hegemonic educational practices and policies are continued barriers for Indigenous youth (Romero-Little et al., 2014). In addition, the contemporary learning environment may also be "unreceptive to culturally diverse learners" (Romero, 1994, p. 53). Often, educators and western academic standards often misinterpret Native behavioral norms as cognitive delays and/or learning deficits, especially bilingual students who continue to be chastised for speaking their Native language in the school setting. This contributes to school systems that have "special education classrooms crowded with Native American D-category students . . . *d*eficit orientation, such as learning *d*isabled, speech *d*elayed, and behavior *d*isorder(ed)" (Romero-Little et al., 2014).

Many of these Native students, parsimoniously categorized as "504s," are placed in special education classrooms as a result of psychological, psychiatric, and educational (school psychologist) evaluations conducted by non-Native professionals.

Unfortunately, these individuals designated as stewards of child mental ability proficiency, capacity, and performance are apt to over-pathologize and are not proficient in conceptualizing examination results within a cultural context, utilizing predominantly deficit-based western approaches. Further, many of the selected psychological, psychiatric, and educational instrumentations used to assess Native students were not normed on the Native population (Verney et al., 2016) and no concessions are made with regard to this important aspect of testing. Also unfortunate are the unitary western standards of intelligence that continue to remain the norm without ethnic and cultural considerations of other forms of intelligence (Romero-Little et al., 2014; Mail et al., 2006; McDonald & Chaney, 2003; Romero, 1994; Tonemah, 1991). In addition, misdiagnosis and over-pathologization by enculturated professionals have resulted in the exceptionally high rate of Native students diagnosed with Attention-Deficit Hyperactivity Disorder (ADHD), borderline intellectual functioning, and unspecified mental illness, combined with educational records indicating limited English proficiency, and low expectations in lifelong special education/individual education plan (IEP) enrollment. These circumstances heavily contribute to the "failure to thrive" in an educational archetype.

Sando (1992) asserted that role-models Native children read about in school "rarely if ever identify with their culture. In fact, nothing in the usual classroom relates to the child's past experiences at home and in the village" (p. 143). This common theme is further exacerbated by having to challenge public school board decisions that exclude the interests of Native students, their families, and their values. This point is simplistically exemplified by parents advocating for the inclusion of Native books in the school library, as occurred within the recent past in an Alaska Native school district whose regional community population was comprised of 81 percent Alaska Native tribal members, as related by a community member in a northwestern Alaska community. These circumstances begin to establish an invisibility and the non-identification for Native students in educational settings that contribute to the foundation for their failure in school. According to Dr. John Aragon, University of New Mexico Cultural Awareness Center, as cited in Sando's *Pueblo Nations* (1992), "Children begin to reject all those things to which they attribute their lack of success: their language, their values learned at home, and their social patterns" (p. 143). Therein begins the impact of trauma-induced acculturation stress for many Native students, with the etiology in an educational institution, from kindergarten through high school, contributing in part to conflicting identity development and potentially contributing to a form of educational neglect. Outside of school, this childhood trauma is further exacerbated by mainstream movies and television programming that romanticize, hypersexualize, or depict savagery of Native peoples (Tehee & Green, 2017), reinforcing stereotypes (e.g. Pocahontas, Little Creek).

Educational Journeys. Within the current educational systems, Indigenous youth are encouraged to leave "home" to pursue higher education and "maintain tribal connections in an increasingly globalized society" (Sumida Huaman et al., 2016, p. 4). These concepts have implications in being a "good Indian and a good student" (Sumida Huaman & Stokes, 2011, p. 3). The complexities of navigating a 21st century education also include an educational system wherein the great majority of teachers of Native students have little credible knowledge about Indigenous "children, families, communities . . . cultures, languages, and contemporary realities" (Romero- Little et al., 2014, p. 179). Thus, well-intentioned teachers approach Indigenous education with the implementation of assimilative instructional methods and may approach the classroom with a savior frame of mind.

Many public school districts in the United States continue to ascribe to an assimilated educational approach, even in districts that serve high Native student populations, such as school districts with

100 percent Native populations (e.g. Alaska), where teachers from the Lower 48 are lured by high-salaried teaching positions to areas with 100 percent Native populations. These educational endeavors are riddled with western-dominated distortions and themes, such as an interpretation of Indian wars being conceptualized as an Indian massacre or cavalry battle (GreyWolf, 2018), told from the government's point of view, with no acknowledgement of Native history, as recounted by Native historians. Sando (1992) asks, "How many dropouts would the reader guess General Sheridan created since he coined the aphorism, 'The only good Indian is a dead Indian'?" (p. 143). Academically, school history books continue to be written from the perspective of the conquerors.

Cultural Patrimony. Academic settings create unnecessary stress and anxiety for Native students. They learn very young that their traditional regalia, items of cultural patrimony, and sacred items are on display and exploited in various forms by history books, science, museums, teachers, and others in educational settings. Students easily observe those items significant to their tribal community and sacrosanct spirituality in a photograph in a school sanctioned American history book, or they may learn that sacred items are being held in a museum, or that their cultural patrimony items are being auctioned off in a public sale. Often these observations yield feelings of internal and community powerlessness toward these injustices against their Native communities.

Feelings of angst create confusion for the Indigenous student and results in manifestations of anger and sadness. These students do not trust in consulting school administrators, staff, or counselors for help because of previous discriminatory treatment (Johnston-Goodstar & VeLure Roholt, 2017). One aspiring psychologist related a vivid middle school memory:

> In 7th grade, I remember I took New Mexico History. In our textbooks was a picture of our dancers in the plaza from like the 1920s or something. I remember I felt so sad to see that in there and felt defeated and confused. Like, how did that happen? I didn't know what to do, so on our last day of school I blacked the picture out with a marker before turning in my textbook. (M. Cheromiah, personal communication, March 19, 2019)

Institutional Racism. Native students, historically and contemporarily, continue to be derided by educators in a multitude of academic settings for wishing to return to serve their tribes or other tribal entity. These students are reminded that their desires and academic pursuits should reflect the American Dream, including amassing great wealth. There is dissonance between the values of the dominant society's educational system and the experience of Indigenous students within those systemic brick and mortar walls. All students are taught about the "Pursuit of Happiness" in the Declaration of Independence. However, the conceptualization of happiness for many Native individuals is not depicted in what dominant society deems fit, resulting in dissonance and identity confusion for many Indigenous students. Anything short of that goal, as propelled by many dominant society educators, is to fail, whether that is through indirect eye contact, inappropriate prosody, culturally inappropriate attire, or hygiene deemed unacceptable. In addition, Johnston-Goodstar and VeLure Roholt (2017) conducted a study depicting the extensive microassaults, microaggressions, and microinsults Native students experience in the school setting. They also documented harsher discipline measures doled out to Native students as compared to their counterparts of other ethnic backgrounds.

Alaska Native Verna Wallis eloquently stated the following of her brother Barry, "After a couple of years of school (at the University of Alaska Fairbanks), he lost interest in sitting in classes and listening to lectures while there were so many things yet to be done in the village, so he came home" (Wallis, 2002, p. 204). In the perceptions of the western world, tribal village life is considered a second-class existence in a third world country. Appallingly, this evaluation of Native village life pervades the judgment of many non-Native professionals working in mental health, educational, political, judicial, and social systems; this prejudice manifests itself in their approach to "fix" the Native child.

Pinnacle. In addition, educational settings where Native children spend the majority of their time continue to present challenges to the navigation of two distinct cultural worlds for many Native students. "Since the white man's arrival, Indian people have struggled to keep their own ways of teaching and learning amidst the dominant society's system of teachers, textbooks, and classrooms" (NICWA, 2016, p. 27);

"the white world told Indians that their ways were bad and worked to destroy their ways" (NICWA, 2016, p. 86). According to Swisher and Tippeconnic (1999), educators utilizing a deficit approach with the goal of assimilation, "remains deeply entrenched in schools" and reflected in "drop-out rates, attendance rates, academic achievement test scores, and enrollment and graduation rates in colleges and universities" (p. 296).

Further, even when Indian students attend college, many of them do not graduate. Bryan McKinley Jones Brayboy, Arizona State University's President's Professor and Borderlands Professor of Indigenous Education and Justice, School of Social Transformation and Center for Indian Education director synopsized, "Only one out of every 5,000 Native Americans and indigenous peoples in the United States who reach the ninth grade will go on to obtain a doctorate" (Terrill, 2018, para. 12). With all the educational challenges that continue to be present for the navigation of a western education, for a Native student, it remains an academic feat for even one in every 5,000 Native students to reach the pinnacle of a higher education degree. Anecdotally, though, the number of those both reaching the educational pinnacle and maintaining traditional ways is increasing.

Left Behind. The first author presented the following narrative in an American Psychological Association (APA) webinar entitled *American Indian, Alaska Native and COVID-19* (17 July 2020) and the information was documented in an APA Division 18, Psychologists in Public Service, newsletter (Ross & GreyWolf, 2020). When the COVID-19 pandemic hit, and school districts transitioned to online classes, many tribal communities were forgotten. As many public school districts boasted to news organizations and other entities that their schools provided Chromebooks to all students in their districts, and that class instruction would be modified or hybrid online, ensuring students' educational standards were met, many Native students fell through the cracks, especially those residing in rural and remote communities.

In the most remote tribal lands, internet access remains elusive, as the infrastructure does not yet exist. In some of these regions, teachers and administrators are also itinerant to the communities. Thus, there was a mass evacuation of these educators when the shelter in place orders were issued. This corresponded to Native children and their parents being left behind in an educational black hole, where no instruction from mandated school curriculum was provided. Likely, once school testing formally resumes, the results will show an even greater disparity in attaining grade level minimum proficiencies and achievements for many of these Native students. In addition, with these parameters in place, these results may skew the outcomes of psychological evaluations by school psychologists and others when assessing grade level abilities.

Pre-College Visits and Tours; Mascots. Higher educational institutions also present unforeseen hurdles for Indigenous students. Native students cannot intellectualize egregious racial profiling they may confront as ethnic minorities in the college setting. In May 2018, while two Mohawk students were touring the Colorado State University campus, they were detained by campus police reportedly because they looked "suspicious" and acted oddly in the campus tour group (Hudetz, 2018). Instead of these Native students completing the tour, they were extracted from the group and escorted to the university police department for arbitration of the situation, including being questioned, having to show identification, and emptying their pockets. This type of prejudice within a systemic institution occurs often, primarily without documented incidents.

Universities and colleges across the nation have only recently, grudgingly, changed their Native mascots to other symbols (LaRocque et al., 2011), revealing the deep prejudice against Native people that lies behind those symbols. This means that Indigenous citizen students have been subjugated to racist and prejudicial attitudes from fellow college students, alumni, and greater college community residents for years. These are merely two examples that discourage Indigenous youth from pursuing higher education, further impacting the dropout rate of Indigenous students.

Termination. Federal Indian policy has also contributed to child maltreatment from time immemorial. In 1991, U.S. Supreme Court Justice Clarence Thomas stated that federal Indian policy is "to say the least, schizophrenic," (Wilkins, 2004, p. 91), which accurately depicts U.S. policy toward Indigenous peoples. At the core of federal Indian policy are the issues of sovereignty, blood quantum, genetic proof, and termination, with which other ethnic groups do not have to contend. AI/AN children become aware of their federal status at various points of maturation, sometimes when they transition from a Bureau of Indian Affairs (BIA) school to a public school or boarding school, or when asked their blood quantum or ethnic identity so a school may be reimbursed for Title IV monies for educating a Native child.

On June 9, 1953, in the 83rd Congress, House Concurrent Resolution (HCR) 108 was introduced to terminate federal supervision of U.S. Native peoples, thus resulting in terminating the status of Indigenous children as U.S. AI/AN citizens. This bill included a proposal to relocate several Midwest tribes. However, the non-participation by one state assisted in defeating the effort. Because of the dependent nature and uncertainty of the status of Indian tribes with the federal U.S. government, AI/AN children must continue to contend with the ways of proving their birthright as written in the laws as it pertains to their tribal and U.S. citizenships. Late in 2018, meetings across the country were convened to address the reorganization of the Department of the Interior (DOI), initiated via short-term notification by U.S. government officials. The DOI retains the authority to alter and transmute matters associated with AI/AN status, recognition as federally recognized tribes, identity (e.g., sociopolitical, eco-psychological, sociocultural, etc.) which are of significant importance to tribal nations and Indigenous People. The U.S. Congress has held the authority to terminate Native U.S. tribes. This is a significant consideration no other populations in the United States have to worry about, and a fact with which tribal leadership across the United States must contend in regard to the welfare of not only their Native children, but all tribal members across the lifespan.

Ecological Considerations. Government policies on exploitation and stripping of natural resources from the land systematically affect the lives of Native children. Many tribal members from a plethora of tribal nations, including children, travelled to Standing Rock, North Dakota to protest the Dakota Access Pipeline (Isaacs et al., 2020; McDonald et al., 2019), which is further explained in chapter 6. The psychological and physical scars Native children will carry into their adolescence and adulthood, born of government-authorized pillaging of the earth, and all the potential fallout will be the weight future generations of Indigenous children will shoulder, in part due to their relationship with Mother Earth. It is unbelievable the pipeline was initially proposed to run near Bismarck, North Dakota. However, it was found to be in propinquity to the city's water sources and residential locations, thus it was relocated to Standing Rock without the same consideration for safety, clean water sources, and the residences of AI families.

As another example, one of the authors was raised in a village where the largest open pit uranium mine was quarried between the 1950s and 1980s. The land still bears the disfigurements of the mining venture today. Some children born during that period were affected physically and neurologically (Shuey et al., 2020) and pregnant women miscarried or had stillborn babies, although the mining companies deny that these outcomes were related to the uranium mining. Now as adults, cancer rates and other ailments correlated with radiation exposure have developed in the population there (Quandelacy, 2010) not only in this community, but in others with uranium mining. Many homes there that Native families occupy today have been assessed for structural stability and the presence of radon. Many of these multigenerational homes located in tribal villages, rural and remote tribal communities, and the sole home for many, have been condemned, displacing families, including children (Shuey et al., 2020).

Current Implications for the Native Child

In a report by the U.S. Department of Health and Human Services, Administration on Children, Youth and Families Children's Bureau documenting 2016 statistical information for AI/AN child maltreatment, they reported the rate of occurrence at 14.2 per 1000 children. However, Willis and Spicer (2013) documented, per the National Center on Child Abuse and Neglect in 1999, that 79.8 percent of AI girls had been sexually abused. With the afore-referenced rates of victimization and child maltreatment in the AI/AN population, there exists a large disparity in the reporting and accuracy of data, in part due to uniformity in reporting among law enforcement, prosecutorial, and judicial, operational definitions, and misclassification of race, and is likely not depicted accurately in state or federal reporting. Although reporting sources maintain inconsistent data, these resources reflect a deficit perspective of Native children and families.

Politics and Law

Child maltreatment by the system is also exacerbated by the emergency response services afforded AI/AN youth. Astonishingly, the AMBER Alert System, the national system set up to help find missing children, was finally signed into law in Indian Country as recently as April 2018. According to the National Crime Information Center (2019), about 7,858 Native children are missing in the United States.

Seamless investigative processes remain deficient at the tribal, state, and federal levels of law enforcement, decreasing the likelihood of prosecution in cases concerning crimes against Indigenous children. This tangible factor also contributes to the epidemic of missing and murdered Indigenous women and girls in the U.S. EchoHawk (2001) surmised:

> [W]ith conflicting jurisdictions, it's easy for children to fall through the cracks. Having federal, tribal and state governments split jurisdiction over offenses occurring in Indian country often leads to duplication, delay, or complete failure in the investigation and prosecution of child sexual abuse cases in Indian country. (p. 97)

Finally, in 2018, a government task force, Operation Lady Justice, was created to address the epidemic of Missing and Murdered Women and Girls (MMIWG) in the United States.

Incarceration Systems

As another complicating factor, the civil and criminal judicial systems create unfair circumstances for Native youth. In 2015, the incarceration rate for the Native population was three times (255 per 1000) that of white youth (83 per 100,000) (Daniel, 2020 [Prison Policy Initiative, n.d.]). Sentencing and penalties for a Native youth are harsher than it would be for a youth of another ethnic minority committing the same crime (Rolnick, 2016). It is not uncommon for Native adolescents in the juvenile justice system to find themselves on a merry-go-round in the judicial system. For example, a Native adolescent in the custody of the Office of Children Services charged with assault in the juvenile justice system could begin their sentenced incarceration at a local juvenile facility, then be shipped out to another facility in the Lower 48 states, be made to attend some sort of treatment for substance use whether or not it was required, be sent back to a facility somewhere in their state of origin, and then be released at the age of eighteen. These conditions are unjust and serve as a precursor to trauma related symptomology in adulthood.

Social systems

Further, the social services systems at different governmental levels persistently contribute to the child maltreatment of AI/AN children. Especially in the more remote and rural areas of Indian Country, child welfare systems may be resistant to responding to a report of abuse or opening a case, or they might be ambivalent about intervening, or they might be overly zealous in opening a case, all of which directly contributes to the systemic maltreatment and neglect of a child. In addition, the likelihood of Indigenous children being removed from their respective family or Native community and being shuffled between community and social service agencies, multiple Native and non-Native family placements, mental health service systems, and judicial entities, without ever receiving mental health treatment, is significantly increased and a reality for many Native children (Ross, 2014). Alternatively, Native children may be sent out of their local tribal region to long-term residential treatment centers in other areas, including across the country or thousands of miles away from home, where they are stripped of all things associated with their Nativeness and are remanded to lengthy programs in excess of eighteen months.

This scenario generates trauma in these Native children, contributing to high rates of post-traumatic stress disorder (PTSD) symptoms upon their return to their communities, reminiscent of the boarding school era when Native children were stolen to fill student quotas. As in the boarding school era, Native parents are without recourse. Attempting to regain custody of their children within this system is difficult at best, in spite of the Indian Child Welfare Act (ICWA). Many of the situations pertaining to the placement of Native children in out-of-region residential treatment centers contribute to the invisibility and namelessness of these Native children, but the trauma they have endured has lasting psychological implications into adulthood, hence institutionalized adverse childhood experiences (ACEs). Reconceptualization of ACEs will be further discussed in chapter 3.

Removal of Native Children. Further complicating this social welfare enigma is the removal of Native children from their families for neglect that is subjectively determined by many non-Native case workers, clinicians, and paraprofessionals who misjudge circumstances through a western lens. This contributes to the unjust placement and adoption of Indigenous children by non-Native families in civil court settings (refer to chapter 4 for further discussion). According to the National Conference of State Legislatures (2020), since 2009, Native children represent the highest number of children in foster care. For many Indigenous families in the United States, there is an underpinning of worry that their children will be removed as a result of a subjective inference by any number of non-Native educators and/or providers, regardless if the parents or guardians are caring for their children well.

Prior to the ICWA of 1978, thousands of Native children were adopted out of Native families and communities through state and private entities to non-Native families. According to the National Indian Child Welfare Act (NICWA) Association (2021), "Research found that 25%–35% of all Native children were being removed; of these, 85% were placed outside of their families and communities— even when fit and willing relatives were available" (para. 1). There are horrific stories nationwide that document the removal of Native children from their families on non-substantiated suspicion of child maltreatment, without corroborated cause. Often the situation under investigation did not need to meet a minimal threshold of reasonable suspicion, or probable cause, which law enforcement officials must ascribe to charge an individual of a crime. Under these circumstances, Native children are removed without cause and there is no recourse for many Native parents. ICWA will be further explored in chapter 4.

Cultural Relevancy

The development and implementation of culturally appropriate treatments for AI/ANs are significant challenges impacting the effective mental health treatment for Native youth. The implementation of cultural conceptualization, or lack thereof, has implications in clinical practice including assessment, diagnosis, and psychological evaluations, as previously referenced in terms of education. Disregarding culture, collectivism, traditional forms of knowledge, and a holistic approach to healing, psychological or medical, this results in the overpathologization of Native children in misdiagnosis, poor treatment prognosis, and other devastating outcomes. Many social science and medical programs continue to ascribe to a one-size-fits-all training and education model in the many behavioral health programs that continue to endorse the notion that all psychological treatments work the same way for all people. People differ in their response to treatment, suggesting the importance of attending to individual differences (Berkman, 2017) when treating them. This holds especially true when non-Native students in secondary education programs and beyond are considering employment in providing treatment services in Indian Country and serving the Native child population.

Dearth of Native Providers

Fortunately, as more ethnic minority scholars are endeavoring to attain higher degrees, specifically, as more Indigenous scholars are obtaining their doctoral degrees, there is a shift in the professional dialogue resulting in a decrease in clinical racism and stigma (e.g., mental health). The Society of Indian Psychologists has affected change within the American Psychological Association (APA) and provided insight through an Indigenous lens. In a multitude of situations, work has been accomplished through allyship. This has occurred through building relationships with individuals and with other ethnic minority groups striving for social justice and willing to dissect and challenge the one-size-fits-all model of western mental health treatment.

Some collegiate institutions have instituted Native focused programs that directly address the parity issues within the field and that facilitate Indigenous scholars' graduation rates nationwide. For example, the University of North Dakota's Indians into Psychology Doctoral Education (INPSYDE) program has awarded approximately thirty-two clinical psychology doctoral degrees since the program's inception in 1992. According to former American Psychological Association Division 45 President and SIP President Justin "Doug" McDonald, currently there exist 150–250 AI/AN psychologists nationwide (personal communication April 28, 2021), thus the ratio of Indigenous psychologists to Native clients has dramatically increased with the projected 2020 Census count (NCAI Policy Research Center, 2021). These concerning statistics highlight the need for continued work to be done, especially in consideration of the systemic challenges in education.

Racism

Child maltreatment also presents itself in general social situations, within communities, border towns, municipalities, schools, and other settings. Unfortunately, long standing stereotypical and prejudicial attitudes persist toward Native children. Bachman (1992) contended:

> As anyone who has lived on or near a reservation . . . can attest, there are countless examples of everyday acts of racism and discrimination. These acts include verbal taunts, jeers, jokes, and racial slurs, which usually stem from prejudice. Parrillo (1995) has defined prejudice as an attitudinal "system of negative beliefs, feelings, and action- orientations regarding a certain group or groups of people." It seems that prejudicial attitudes are quite well established, particularly among whites who live in close proximity to American Indians. Unfortunately, once established, these prejudgments are difficult to eradicate and continue in the same or more virulent form from generation to generation.

In an effort to prepare AI/AN children for racist conflict, Native families should discuss historical traumas, stressors, and discrimination. Research demonstrates that children and youth who are taught about racial barriers and difficulties in this way have more positive mental health reserves than youth who are not (Bowman & Howard, 1985).

Religious Practices

The U.S. government also aimed to control AI/AN people, including children, through religion. The underlying assumption was that AI/AN would fit better with the immigrants' schemes for the New World if they practiced a "real" religion and gave up their savage religious customs (Tafoya & Del Vecchio, 2005). Many tribes took the practice of their religion underground and did not share the intricacies with outsiders due to the extermination and exploitation of many years of attempted religious genocide levied toward tribes and tribal members (Ross, 2018). Despite the passage of the American Indian Religious Freedom Act in 1978, tribal entities continue to remain cautious. Children are instructed very early of the importance of silence pertaining to religious practices. In some tribes, customs dictate select young members partake in ceremonial learning for several years, which precludes attendance in a mainstream school. This education in traditional knowledge has been used as a basis for psychologists and educators as a means of pathologizing a child for presentation of delusions, hallucinations, or other pathology associated with traditional religious practices.

Recovering Our Loved Ones

Although individuals in mainstream society may not conceptualize the repatriation of ancestral remains or return of items of cultural patrimony as child maltreatment in the Native child population, the relationship with ancestors, past and present, and ceremonial items with Native traditional religious connotations, are consequential to the overall well-being of the tribe, including children. The repatriation of Native ancestral remains, ranging in age from elders to infants, and items of cultural patrimony held for decades in institutions and government warehouses have taken its toll. These unauthorized removals have caused irreparable harm to tribal members, in consideration of critical components with spiritual implications.

These acts of pilfering constitute child maltreatment as intergenerational psychological scarring has been the result of thefts, unlawful removal, grave robbing, and outright burglary of their ancestors' bodies and ceremonial items under the justification of scientific knowledge. Many children have witnessed the return of their ancestor's remains and sacred ceremonial items through physically awaiting their return (Robbins, 1999; Thomas, 2000), through ceremonial activities for restoration and/or burial, and through being a part of community and family discussions. Some tribes have struggled with repatriation ceremonies related to reburial (Preucel & Pecos, 2015; Thomas, 2000). William Tallbull, Northern Cheyenne, posed the question:

How would you feel if your grandmother's grave were opened and the contents were shipped back east to be boxed and warehoused with 31,000 others and itinerant pothunters were allowed to ransack her house in search of "artifacts" with the blessing of the U.S. government? It is un-Christian. It is (now) punishable by law. (Thomas, 2000, p. 214)

In 1990, the Native American Graves Protection and Repatriation Act (NAGPRA), 25 USC. 3005, was passed by Congress and signed into law. Mind you, this was not to afford U.S. Native Peoples special rights, "NAGPRA awards an equal protection of property rights already extended to other Americans" (Thomas, 2000, p. 215). A 1999 *New York Times* story by Catherine Robbins depicted Native children from a southwest population asking questions in a classroom about the repatriation process and the remains of their ancestors. These children were left to contend with questions about the value of their lives as Native People, their culture, and their livelihood, as they contemplated how these callous acts were sanctioned by the government prior to NAGPRA. The return of ancestors and traditional items constitutes child maltreatment in that Native children are exposed to reprehensible historical acts which have implications in identity formation, anxiety, depression, and stress-related symptoms, contemporarily.

Summary

Based upon the afore-referenced circumstances and systemic injustices, the literature indicates that measures of individual health and wellbeing among AI/AN children and youth were disparaging (Rolnick, 2016; Campbell & Evans-Campbell, 2011). Circumstances related to adolescent substance use will be addressed in chapter 3. The afore-referenced information and statistics contained in this chapter are reflective of the multitude of abuses and injustices that the U.S. Native population has endured. One must ponder with whom and where the culpability of child maltreatment in the Native population resides.

It is important to understand that the mental health of Native youth (and the lived experiences of AI/AN People in general) is steeped in historical trauma and oppression, and requires a complex set of coping skills that parents can help convey (Campbell & Evans-Campbell, 2011). AI/AN adults can further support their children contending with oppression and discrimination through ethnic and group socialization as well as through cultural retraditionalism and revitalization within their communities. Regardless of all these systemic factors diminishing tribal identity, the Native population, hence the Native child, remains resilient.

Postulating the logic and rationale behind the resilience of Native youth, despite disparaging health and well-being outcome analyses, Dr. Iva GreyWolf championed, "The very things that are a part of our (Native) lifestyle are what sustain us; a sense of community and perseverance" (personal communication, May 22, 2019). Perseverance is a characteristic Native youth learn and develop from an early age (I. GreyWolf, personal communication May 22, 2019) and is a protective factor. "Living your creation story" (G. Vigil, personal communication, May 22, 2019), may also be a significant contributing factor to Native resilience. For Native youth residing outside the boundaries of tribal lands, community is also an important and protective factor. Hypothetically, this referent resilience may be embedded in epigenetics (Pember, 2016; Brockie et al., 2013, Brave Heart & DeBruyn, 1998) wherein there is an inherent recessive gene demarcating resiliency, passed through generations. According to Dr. Joseph Gone, *Aaniiih-Gros Ventre* of Montana, "Native peoples' ability to maintain culture and sense of who they are in the face of such a traumatic history suggests an inherited resilience that bears scientific examination" (Pember, 2016). This DNA component, along with the horrific historical, political, social, physical, biological, and psychological circumstances to which the Native population has been subjected, may be correlated with resiliency in the Native child.

3

Protective and Risk Factors

We are free to be who We are—to
create Our own life out of the past
and out of the present. We are
Our ancestors. When We can
heal ourselves, We also heal Our
ancestors, Our Grandmothers,
Our Grandfathers, and Our
children. When We heal ourselves,
We heal Mother Earth.
—Dr. Rita Pitka Blumenstein,
    First certified Alaska Native
    tribal doctor

The overall health and mental well-being of the Native child is nested
in the simplicity of balance in the holistic realms of the mind, body,
and spirit with relational connectedness in the cosmological and the
ecological spheres. "According to many Indian definitions, ... one's
mental state exists in balance with other aspects of the self. It is not
necessarily distinct from the social, emotional, and spiritual components comprising the whole individual" (Nelson & Manson, 2000,
pp. 311–312). The compilation of these aspects sets the foundation for a

Native child's worldview, values, beliefs, morality, and guides the *way of life* or *way of being*. Unfortunately, this all-encompassing Indigenous way of existing, sometimes referred to as "The Indian Problem" or "White Man's Burden" (McDonald & Chaney, 2003, p. 39) has conflicted with dominant society's ideological constitutions since contact. Tragically, the relational way of life Native Peoples valued was repeatedly assailed upon contact and throughout U.S. history (Kawagely, 2006; Minthorn, 2018). Oppressive sentiments and microaggressions directed toward Native peoples continue into present times.

Rewriting the Narrative

In Our Own Words

Native scholars in many disciplines are now challenging this disparaging dialogue about Native Peoples and changing the literature to accurately reflect the Native perspective (Lyons, 2000). This has significant implications for the 29 percent of the overall AI/AN youth who are under the age of eighteen (National Congress of American Indians [NCAI], 2021b). In her article, "For the Love of Our Children: An Indigenous Connectedness Framework", Jessica Saniguq Ullrich documented how connectedness was related to protective factors associated with traditional and contemporary tenets for Native youth. She noted "the disruption of connectedness has been harmful to everyone, not just Indigenous communities" (2019, p. 1). Another example of adding Native authenticity to the literature was a study by Goodluck and Willeto (2009) that was conducted with several tribal populations, wherein they identified a series of shared protective factors.

In opposition to these strength-based studies, an official U.S. government study about the health and well-being of AI/AN children depicted the Native child's status as bleak and hopeless as it pertained to the plethora of categories surveyed (U.S. Department of Health and Human Services [USDHHS], 2013). However, when scrutinizing this parental report, there are multiple caveats based on western empiricism that significantly contribute to this destructive construal of the assessment of the health and well-being of Native children. For example, out of 91,642 children, only 1,465 parents or guardians were surveyed by phone about the status of their children, omitting a large swath of families. Nevertheless, the results gained from this small survey group are applied to the entire Native child population. The report admitted that "the findings of this report may contain sources of unintended bias" (USDHHS, 2013, p. 6), including legal requirements that may not have been met to satisfy enrollment requirements for AI/AN race/ethnicity, and in the cultural irrelevance as well as applicability of some of the items surveyed. Yet, the biased report stands as a reflection of an overall dismal status of AI/AN children. Negative reports and information on AI/AN children are predominant in the mainstream literature, while there is a dearth of positive health and well-being literature pertaining to the Native child population (Willeto, 2014).

Therefore, in working with Native youth, in any capacity, there is an inherent responsibility to inspect, analyze, and interpret reports, articles, and literature with caution (McDonald et al., 1993). The reader also bears the responsibility of further examining the protective factors associated with the overall well-being of the AI/AN child, from the perspective of Native scholars, professionals, and those that approach this conceptualization with a strengths-based approach. The educator, counselor, or systemic/institutional representative has an imperative duty to examine the protective factors *within* a cultural context, as not doing so has had detrimental effects for the Native child throughout U.S. history. These cultural protective factors have long been discarded as irrelevant or insubstantial when an initial assessment has been conducted or during a first encounter when the professional initially meets a Native child and/or Native family.

Currently, these factors signifying culturally relevant strengths, in general, are not deemed to be protective factors from a western perspective. For example, a Native child residing with a grandparent or relative is often characterized as coming from a dysfunctional or defective family background for merely being raised by an individual outside of the nuclear family unit, as viewed from an enculturated perspective. In the context of an Indigenous collective community, this is a cultural norm and viewed as a strength, as the multiplicity of family relations enriches the child's upbringing. Another common example refers to AI/AN children who do not maintain eye contact or do not look a non-Native adult in the eyes when being addressed, or a Native child who refuses to speak, or speaks in a low, subdued tone. From a western perspective, children exhibiting these traits are automatically deemed resistant, unengaged, ambivalent, cognitively delayed, or pathologized, as these characteristics do not "fit" into dominant society's norms. Instead, within a cultural context, a Native child not looking an elder (as all providers will be) in the eyes is a sign of respect. Speaking slowly or quietly, a cultural norm, is also considered culturally appropriate.

Furthermore, a child refusing to communicate with the professional or another adult may be considered a protective factor, as speaking up or the misinterpretation of their words in a prior setting may have resulted in a horrendous outcome for the child or the child's family in a previous experience (e.g., disciplinary action, hospitalization, or removal from a classroom, home, or family). Additionally, it should be noted, secrecy has been a vital practice for the preservation of Indigenous cultural knowledge, so a Native child may not share all aspects of their acquired knowledge as instructed at an early age. This practice often rivals the authority of non-Native adults, practitioners, and educators, resulting in Native children being forced to speak, share, and converse against their will. This scenario, which occurs all too often, quickly builds systemic, institutional, and governmental distrust in Native children, parents, families, and communities. This may further exacerbate an already healthy general mistrust of outside providers and institutions based on similar intergenerational negative experiences (Campbell & Evans-Campbell, 2011).

In 2005, Dr. Bryan McKinley Jones Brayboy published an article, "Toward a Tribal Critical (TribalCrit) Race Theory in Education." In TribalCrit, he introduced nine tenets that will be used throughout the following sections to explain how issues confronted by Indigenous populations are reframed and contextualized from a Native perspective. Although TribalCrit was originally applied to western education systems, these tenets relate to the colonialistic ideology that infiltrates Indigenous epistemologies, pedagogies, ontologies, sovereignty, identities, families, languages, lands, and self-determination.

Native Identity and Identification

Today, Indigenous identity and identification are convoluted, which constitutes an entire dissertation unto its own, and beyond the scope of this book. However, in dissecting and scrutinizing Native identity and identification, one must ask, "Who is Native?" (McDonald et al., 2018). The basis of assessing an individual's cultural identity or identification should not be a person's phenotype (Brayboy, 2005; McDonald et al., 2019). From indications of the AI/AN population in the 2020 U.S. Census (NCAI Policy Research Center, 2021) and 2010 U.S. Census (2012), which were by self-report, hence self-identification, 3.7 million (NCAI Policy Research Center, 2021) versus 2.9 million (2010, U.S. Census) people identified as being AI/AN alone and 5.9 million (NCAI Policy Research Center, 2021) versus 2.3 million (2010, US Census) people identified as being mixed AI/AN. In Brayboy's (2005) "Tribal Critical Race Theory," the fourth tenet stated, "Indigenous peoples have a desire to obtain and forge tribal sovereignty, tribal autonomy, self-determination, and self-identification" (p. 429). This takes into consideration ethnic fraud, but also emphasizes the point Indigenous People should have the right to make this determination ourselves. Currently, the U.S. government decides who is eligible as a beneficiary of treaty rights and services based on blood quantum.

We will briefly highlight some quantitative research conducted by several Native scholars affirming robust cultural identity and identification. In two sample populations in different U.S. regions, the researchers found that a Native person's satisfaction with life does not correlate with their level of acculturation. Different levels of identification (e.g., traditional, bicultural, assimilated, marginalized) did not overall correlate with these Native individuals' self-report in being satisfied with the circumstances of their lives (Prairie Chicken, 2019; Ross, 2018). In a study of an Alaskan Yup'ik population aged fourteen to ninety-four, in which they either ascribed to a Yup'ik lifestyle and values [enculturation], or a "Kass'aq [white] way of life [acculturation]" (Wolsko et al., 2007, p. 54), participants reported higher degrees of happiness, better coping, and less substance abuse if they ascribed to the Yup'ik lifestyle. Early research with Native youth based in an "Orthogonal Cultural Identification Theory" (Oetting & Beauvais, 1991), wherein identification with one culture does not detract from identification with another culture, posits that overall health and well-being may be affected by levels of acculturation. Subsequent research rooted in an Orthogonal Theory of Biculturalism (McDonald et al., 2016) used American Indian Cultural Identification (AICI) and European American Cultural Identification (EACI) as factors in four types of identification: traditional, bicultural, assimilated, and marginalized. This theory postulated that individuals identifying as bicultural (high traditional and high European identification) have higher levels of adaptive functioning in comparison to those identifying as marginalized (low traditional and low European identification) and experience higher levels of psychopathology (Gorneau, 2002; Martell et al., 2020; McDonald et al. 2016; McDonald et al., 2019; Oetting & Beauvais, 1991; Ross, 2014).

Identity and identification can become risk factors for, and have implications in, child maltreatment, in the further convolution of the identity of a child. Recurrent offensive and racist messages directed toward Native youth can unsettle an otherwise well-adjusted, confident child. It can have devastating effects for a Native child to be repeatedly told or oppressively teased, "You are not Native enough," or to hear as a slur or put down, "You're too Native." Cognitive assaults can be internalized and further complicated by the dominant society's generational propaganda against Native people (McDonald et al., 2019), and can translate into self-deprecating thoughts for youth, such as, "You're never going to be good enough." From a psychological standpoint, individuals tend to believe the thoughts that recur most often and consequently behave accordingly (McDonald et al., 2019).

This afore-referenced trailblazing empirical research into Native identity and identification is a start toward examination of these constructs. It also establishes an intersection between clinical, community, cultural, and indigenous psychologies, further regenerating discussion about indigeneity with the AI/AN population, including Native children. Thus, future research conducted by scholars, through an imperative Indigenous lens, within a community-based participatory paradigm, will greatly inform the dialogue about Indigenous youth identity and identification. However, determination of tribal membership, as iterated, should be left to tribal nations.

Resilience

Native scholars have undertaken the concept of resilience and contextualized the construct from an Indigenous lens. The word "resilience" is often used from a dominant society perspective with Native Peoples with an air of casualness. In some circles, Native individuals have pushed back on the use of the term, as it has been used to a point where it can be patronizing or convey an ordinariness, without acknowledgement of 500 years of an oppressive history. When used authentically, or through an Indigenous contextualization, the essence of resilience acknowledges Our history.

Minthorn (2018) discussed resiliency in the battles the ancestors endured stating, "Because of the resilience and fight of our ancestors in battle, we are here today" (p. 67). These battles may be construed as actual warfare throughout history, or contemporary litigation pertaining to water rights, land rights, education, repatriation of ancestors or cultural artifacts, and the legal wars to protect our children, families, and communities. BigFoot and GreyWolf (2014) discussed resiliency demarcation rests in Indigenous traditions. Dr. B.M.J. Brayboy expounded on the concept of individual, familial, and communal resiliency. He discussed the term implies some form of presence of trauma one must be "resilient in the face of," but also cogitated whether resilience "requires a constant state of trauma" (personal communication, March 10, 2021). Due to the collectivistic nature of Native communities and the interwoven relationships therein, traumas, oppression, and stressors have a greater negative effect (BigFoot & GreyWolf, 2014).

Dr. Brayboy legitimized Native history in resilience stating, "The fact that we are still around and the fact that we adapt and we adjust is absolutely crucial to our survival and always has been, but it also acknowledges the terms of the debate that says there's a constancy of bad things happening to us that we have to be resilient from" (personal communication, March 10 2021). In reframing the concept, Dr. Brayboy stated in resilience "folks are finding ways to engage in well-being and meaningful relations with one another who recognize the responsibilities in those relationships, but are also then working towards some common set of good" (personal communication, March 10, 2021).

Protective Factors

Highly protective factors for Native families and children include their culture (Gordon & Roberts, 2021; Willeto, 2014; Wolsko et al., 2007), cultural knowledge and traditions (Gone, 2019; McDonald et al., 1993), inclusive of stories and storytelling (BigFoot & GreyWolf, 2014;

Brayboy, 2005), ceremonies (Bigfoot & GreyWolf, 2014; Gone, 2019), spirituality (Goodluck & Willeto, 2009; McDonald et al., 2019), language (Goodluck & Willeto, 2009; Preucel & Pecos, 2015; Ross, 2018), altruism and philanthropy (BigFoot & GreyWolf, 2014), and the extended family (Goodluck & Willeto, 2009; McDonald et al., 1993), wrapped in the sanctuary of interconnectedness (Gordon & Roberts, 2021; Ullrich, 2019), relationality (Kawagley, 2006; McDonald et al., 1993; Moorehead et al., 2015; Naranjo, 2017), and respect (Kawagley, 2006). Of course, these protective factors are the compositional foundation of the identity of the Native child. Contextualized from a Native standpoint, these components of identity are impossible to compartmentalize and exist relationally with each other. The intertwining of these elements is the exemplification of the durability in present-day Native children, families, and communities. These protective factors in the context of Brayboy's fifth tenet of TribalCrit (2005) asserts, "The concepts of culture, knowledge, and power take on new meaning when examined through an Indigenous lens" (p. 429), thus will be introduced through this lens.

Spirituality

The delineation between religion and spirituality often presents as confusing for many outsiders as the constructs are difficult to conceptualize from a western lens as separate frameworks. In actuality, "many Indians feel that spirituality is the core of being Indian, a core which has remained intact because it has been kept private and sometimes hidden" (Swinomish Tribal Mental Health Project, 1991, p. 131). Spirituality for Native Peoples is a very private affair, which in part is based in the demoralization and demonization of Native traditional religions from contact through the Indian Religious Act of 1978. In the late 19th century, Native traditional religious practices were outlawed, thus maintaining secrecy and annexing traditional Native practices underground preserved traditional religious ways of life (BigFoot & GreyWolf, 2014; Ross, 2018).

Wildcat (2001) articulated the distinction between religion and spirituality. He intimated that spirituality was not reducible to materialistic mechanics and not based in objects or logic, which may be applied to the construct of religion. Sando (1992) asserted there was no word for religion. George Tinker, an Osage theologian, stated:

Most adherents of traditional American Indian ways characteristically deny that their people ever engaged in any religion at all. . . . Their whole culture and social structure was and still is infused with a spirituality that cannot be separated from the rest of the community's life at any point. (Deloria & Wildcat, 2001, p. 54)

Many Native Peoples assert that spirits are present in all things (McDonald et al., 2019). Further, there is a strong relationality between a person and the spirits that are present at all times, thus one is never alone. Relationality also extends to nature, land formations and places, the universe, and animals. Thus, these concepts contest the constructs of visual and auditory hallucinations, delusions, and animism, which are often perceived in western psychological science as pathological. Former Hualapai Nation Tribal Court Judge Joseph Flies-Away stated, "Spirituality helps to connect and bind us to each other as a community, as a tribe and as a nation. It clarifies relationships and is what makes healing happen" (Mirsky, 2004, p. 5).

Simplistically, several main differences between Native spirituality and western organized religions are illustrated in the contrast of free sharing of biblical philosophy and canons. Western religions exercise proselytizing, ecumenism, written words (bibles or other religious books), hierarchical doctrines, penance, and monetary tithing or offerings, which are not components of Indigenous spirituality.

Traditional Ways of Knowing/Culture/Ceremony

Much as spirituality and religious knowledge are protected, ceremony and traditional knowledge are safeguarded, attributed to religious genocide and exploitation by outsiders. As referenced earlier, children are instructed early on not to share this knowledge outside Indigenous circles. From a very early age, Native children are generally educated and immersed in traditional practices (Naranjo, 2017). Whether this knowledge was derived from observation, practice, or apprenticeship, children are also instructed about their roles in the community (Romero-Little, 2011). They are reminded to never forget who they are and where they come from. This powerful message is ingrained in daily living, and also affirmed through socioecological relations, as "culture is rooted to lands on which they live as well as to their ancestors who lived on those lands before them" (Brayboy,

2005, p. 434). These lands are sacred and also where ceremonies are conducted.

Gone (2019) discussed ceremony as a sacrifice and constituted it as a "therapeutic resource" (p. 3), which ameliorated substance use. Gone (2019) also noted that "colonial anomie" and ceremonial tradition disruption contributed to psychopathology. Thus, BigFoot's (2020) refined meaning of the significance of ceremony becomes sharper:

> Ceremony was used to make it through difficult times and then afterwards to express gratitude. When you take away something that was a part of the society like ceremony, in many levels and degrees people lose their way of coping that allows them to thrive, feel whole, and balanced. (p. 12)

Thus, if a Native youth experiences holism and balance through ceremony, negative feelings are mitigated. Chandler & Lalonde (2008, as cited in Willeto, 2014), found that Native youth were sheltered against suicide risk through cultural preservation. Cultural preservation can include, but is not limited to, participation in traditional roles and activities, engaging in traditional forms of expression, and interactions with extended family and community members centered in traditional language conversation and tribal values.

Altruism, Philanthropy, and Interconnectedness

A core traditional value is centered in what would be altruism and philanthropy, or selfless generosity in giving. While BigFoot and GreyWolf (2014) shared that giving of oneself through storytelling assists in transcending trauma for women, storytelling serves as a protective factor for all genders across the lifespan. Stories illuminate community dynamics and serve as individual responsibility reminders of survival in the community (Brayboy, 2005). "Survivors, descendants, family, and community members hold our stories close to the heart. Stories shape us, uplift us, hurt us. They constrain and free. Stories are shared, repeated, circulated, passed down generations" (Lomawaima, 2018, p. 12). Through stories, Native women engage in cultural storytelling, assisting with Native practices, and modeling behaviors that are traditionally expected (BigFoot & GreyWolf, 2014); this act of giving bridges relationships with various family and community members, thus expanding connectivity with others at a greater community level.

Values of philanthropy and altruism support the community, the family, and the individual (Ross, 2018) and not only builds, but sustains connectedness in a multiplicity of intergenerational relationships for the child (peer, adult, elder). Gordon and Roberts (2021) assert connectedness was a protective factor as it pertained to victimization and violence. They noted the components of connectedness in the integration of cultural activities and family were significant in fortifying community bonds. In another sense, Brayboy discussed altruism in Native students attaining a higher education, as their knowledge was to be used selflessly for purposes exceeding individual benefit of the educational degree; the acquired knowledge would be employed for the benefit of the Native community (personal communication, March 10, 2021).

Language and Relatedness

The language of many Native nations serves to establish the People as a people and shape the identity of a Native person. Native languages are used for the intergenerational transmission of knowledge, beliefs, values, culture, and stories (Goodluck & Willeto, 2009). Traditional languages possess life and convey relatedness between all spiritual and living beings. According to R. Pecos (2020),

> Language has a spirit, and it must be nurtured to fulfill its purpose, to thrive in its existence, to flourish in its role, to be vibrant in its contribution, bringing other living spirits to life into a world of coexistence and interdependence. (p. 13)

The significance of language has been iterated throughout Indigenous literature, thus prohibition and termination of the use of Native languages has had a significant impact on the identity and self-valuation of Nativeness. A Native elder in the southwest imparted the following, "It is the language that carries the nature and character of who we are and how we are related to one another, and to Mother Earth, and to all the things we experience in life. Once we've lost that, we have lost everything" (Preucel & Pecos, 2015, p. 234). Thus, today, parents, learning environments, and communities fostering Native language retention and language use bridge the global belongingness of the child's place and reestablish those missing intergenerational components of interrelatedness. Early interventions in language revitalization have been shown to be a protective factor in program development (Sims, 2021) and a way to reverse dislocating influences (Willis & Spicer, 2013).

Some Indigenous languages in existence today are considered linguistic isolates, connoting that the language is not related to any other language family (Campbell, 2017; Crystal, 1997) in the world. After the boarding school era, between 1970–1990, there was a shift toward primary English use in the United States educational system with children entering school and in the pre-kindergarten population (Sims, 2021). This further reduction in Native language use by a much younger generation suggests the further breakdown of interrelated relationships and an increase in parsimonious perspective. Tribal nations across the United States have countered this by beginning to fully exercise their self-determination in traditional language revitalization efforts, thus enhancing and restoring critical pieces of identity. For example, one southwest state acquiesced to the tribes the ability to certify Indigenous language teachers as their sovereign right and because neither the state nor any of its educational institutions had the capacity to certify tribal languages (R. Pecos, personal communication, September 30, 2020).

Critical Examination

The aforementioned protective factors have contributed to the strengthening of Native children and their families as they navigate challenging circumstances, including institutional and systemic racism. These protective factors sustain Indigenous individuals, families, and communities. It is critical to also examine the common risk factors impacting Native children and their families before conferring on resolutions.

Risk Factors

Colonialism and Poverty

In the "Touchstones of Hope" webinar, hosted by the National Indian Child Welfare Association, Mr. Terry Cross posited there were several factors needed for colonialism to succeed, which would also be considered high risk factors for Indigenous children. These factors included: "Take territory—land; take natural resources—energy/food; take sovereignty—disrupt leadership and governance; take away the legitimacy of thought—worldview, language, spirituality, healing; take the children" (Cross, 2020). In terms of the sociopolitical history of Indigenous Peoples, these factors have generally been the basis of assimilative efforts used by governmental, institutional, and educational entities. The first TribalCrit tenet states, "Colonization is endemic to society" (Brayboy, 2005). Thus, the results of colonialistic thought, policy, and governance have led to detrimental outcomes in psychological, medical, and social arenas for Native children and families.

Colonialism aims to impact and pervade every aspect of Native life. Poverty permeates the lives of AI/AN youth. NCAI documented the estimated poverty rates for the AI/AN population in 2017 as 26.8 percent in comparison to the nation at 14.6 percent as a whole (2021) based upon U.S. Census data. NCAI also reported the median household income for AI/ANs at $40,315 as compared to the nation at $57,652 as a whole (2021). The combination of the afore-referenced integration of colonialistic policies, high rates of poverty in Native communities, and increased rates of toxic stress set the stage for increased health, social, and medical risk factors for Native families and children. Thus, the ways that we push back against these multisystemic, multistrata calculated strategies includes activism in, and advocation for, social justice reform resulting in local, municipal, state, regional, and national policy, procedure, and systemic change. In the following sections, we further examine these risk factors.

Education

Education was always a part of the Native way of life (Deloria & Wildcat, 2001; McDonald et al., 2018; Romero-Little, 2011). Traditional systems of education have always been in place and the facilitation of knowledge was practiced over thousands of years (B. Brayboy, personal communication, 2021; Kawagely, 2006; Sando, 1992). The family, tribe, clan and responsible mentors educated members of the community, including the youth, until tasks were clearly learned and apprentices were proficient. Traditional education was an essential component of daily life and ceremonies; they were not to be isolated activities (Demmert, 2001, 2011), and this education was for survival of the tribal community. Changes in education were a result of cultural, social, and political interventions that have taken place among Native peoples (Demmert, 2001, 2011). The introduction of missionaries and formal educational opportunities offering religious curriculums as well as exposure to new technologies (Demmert, 2001, 2011). The introduction of the American educational system (e.g., boarding schools) is most associated with institutional racism, trauma, and colonization.

Currently, with regard to overall well-being, Sando (1992) posited that Native children generally have a well-established positive self-concept until about the time they start school. This point bears significant examination as Native students nearing the end of elementary school "begin to withdraw, becoming sullen, resistant, and indolent" (Garrett & Pichette, 2000, p. 7) which may represent the dissonance in two incompatible cultural worlds. For many Native students, school does not have positive connotations. Hill et al. (2010) surmised that for some Native students,

> Their very survival depended upon their ability to know how to deal with and live in both the White world and their own. The struggles, tension, and difficulties this creates are enormous as persons negotiate expectations and obligations they have in two incompatible worlds. The shifting this requires also makes it very difficult to maintain a strong sense of balance and harmony in one's life. (p. 21)

In consideration of school, a strong emphasis by the authors has been obstinately placed on this element of a Native child's life during those critical formative years. This setting is where children spend the majority of their time, both in years and number of daily hours, as mandated by law. Dr. B.M.J. Brayboy opined that the school system is "actually working as it was designed" (personal communication, March 10, 2021). Western education has been a derisive element of assimilation, hence colonialism, and as a result, positioned many Native children as liabilities and in "at risk" categories. According to Mr. Regis Pecos,

> It is to our collective best interest to enlarge our worlds to appreciate one another. Western education forces us to marginalize [ourselves] into a system that has never accepted us . . . being in a fragile point . . . that's necessary in this time to reclaim and recapture and reground

ourselves so that we don't contribute to that ultimate disconnect. (Personal communication, September 30, 2020)

Assimilation

School attendance is also mandated by law. For many Native students, there is very little recourse as it pertains to public school education options and due to the socioeconomic status of many Native families, opportunities for private school education are negligible. For Native children, the institution of school and its curriculum have not changed since 1890 (R. Pecos, personal communication, September 30, 2020) and its purpose, to "eradicate Indianness" (Brayboy, 2005, p. 437) and assimilate Native children into dominant culture (Johnston-Goodstar & VeLure Roholt, 2017), has been the everlasting goal. This goal aligns with Dr. Brayboy's (2005) sixth tenet of TribalCrit: "Governmental policies and educational policies toward Indigenous peoples are intimately linked around the problematic goal of assimilation" (p. 429). Western education programs at all levels, beginning with pre-K, as iterated, have focused on western themes, western history, and invalidated anything Indigenous.

This fact, unto itself, is a risk factor for many Native children. There is a focused intentionality of the school system to deconstruct the Native identity. Unless the methodologies of public education change, the approaches in public school teaching change, and the sociopolitical circumstances related to aspects of school governance change, very little will change with regard to educational outcomes for the Native child. This aspect of homeostasis leads one to wonder if the school system, by design, has a continued intent to homogenize Native students, with a continued resistance to multiculturalism (Gone, 2011; McDonald and Chaney, 2003) and the continued incorporation and assimilation of Native Peoples into the American population.

The usual response by educators and public school systems has been to blame the Native parents and tribal communities for the failures of the Native child in the school system, related to maintaining their culture and traditions. Interestingly, in 2020, Presidential Executive Order 13950 "Combating Race and Sex Stereotyping" banned all diversity initiatives in government and state entities that receive government funding in the United States (Delaney & Thompson, 2020). This order further perpetuated homogenization and homeostasis. Fortunately, the executive order was rescinded on January 20,

2021, when President Joe Biden took office (Rennie et al., 2021). However, the emotional distress and psychological stress experienced and carried by federal, state, city, and tribal workers will take time to repair and heal.

Mr. Regis Pecos, a traditionalist from Cochiti Pueblo, who previously served the State of New Mexico for twenty-five years in various capacities and currently serves as a legislative senior policy advisor, discussed with the first author circumstances in the very early years of school where adverse childhood experiences (ACEs) could become a contributor to one part of an added marginalization in school for Native students. Remarkably, researchers are beginning to advocate for the inclusion of historical trauma (Brockie et al., 2013; Warne & Lajimodiere, 2015; Winters & Winters, 2020) as an ACE risk factor. Mr. Pecos described unfavorable educational conditions wherein Native children are pushed out of the school system due to disciplinary factors, as a result of systemic failures (which have been addressed extensively in chapter 2), and their tribes lack support to get these students back on track. These circumstances, where students are judged by school administrators and classified as incorrigible as early as elementary school, can further lead to a school to prison pipeline, which becomes an abrupt reality. In an article entitled, "'Our Kids Aren't Dropping Out; They're Being Pushed Out': Native American Students and Racial Microaggressions in Schools," Johnston-Goodstar and VeLure Roholt (2017) discussed contemporary detrimental factors related to public school attendance. Some of these factors were related to incidents wherein Native students were subjected to microinsults, microassaults, and microinvalidations (See DeAngelis, 2009 for definitions) in the educational setting by teachers, administrators, coaches, counselors, and in extracurricular settings via racial slurs and other discriminatory behaviors.

Educators and Governance

Additionally, the risk paradigm in educational settings increases as it relates to the educators in schools. Rarely, if ever, for the duration of a Native child's educational career, will the child encounter a Native educator. According to Mr. Pecos, fifty years ago, only 1 percent of teachers teaching Native youth in public schools were Native educators. Today, that statistic has only increased to 2 percent. Thus, investment in higher education must be a priority, and funding infrastructure must be established (R. Pecos, personal communication, September 30, 2020). Furthermore, as Mr. Pecos iterated, there is minimal or no Native representation in the governance of schools, inclusive of school boards and administrators, to help drive school policy. Thus, there are no policies or programs developed to meet the unique needs of Native students (R. Pecos, personal communication, September 30, 2020). In navigating school challenges, Native students must depend heavily on their established traditional and secular protective factors, rely on elements of their Native identities, their personal resiliency, and perform four times as hard as non-Native peers to beat the odds so they can matriculate and graduate.

Exclusion of Culture

This was exemplified in a non-Native administrator's macro-illustration of school success, observed by the first author in a remote village where all the students were Native, and the administrators and teachers were all non-Native. The drawing included home, school, and community, with no inclusion of culture. One of the most important factors for the success of Native children in school is the inclusion of culture. But, as with most public school operations, culture is largely neglected, resisted, and excluded from the Native child's education. The NCAI Youth Commission (2018) issued a press statement: "To show respect to cultures and spiritual beliefs of tribal nations, public schools should protect and preserve the traditional religious rights and cultural practices of American Indians and Alaska Natives in the way the American Indian Religious Freedom Act intended" (para. 3). In reflection, should the wearing of traditional regalia by Native students at public school graduation ceremonies cause an uproar? On April 26, 2019, due to the disallowance and disrespect by school administrations across the U.S. for decades, the Society of Indian Psychologists (SIP) issued a position statement in support of Native students wearing their traditional Native regalia during graduation ceremonies. SIP iterated:

> The First Amendment of the Constitution of the United States
> promotes freedom of religion and prohibits the restriction of religious
> practices, and the American Indian Religious Freedom Act recon-
> firmed that those protections apply to Native American religious
> practices. Native religious practices, such as possession of sacred

objects, traditions, and sacred rites are generally accepted as sufficiently religious under the first amendment freedoms.

SIP supported Native students being able to wear traditional regalia and accoutrements such as an eagle feather attached to their mortar board and beaded items. They also made recommendations for inclusive language that schools might use to incorporate in school policies (SIP, 2019).

Intersection of Mental Health, Identity, and Maladaptive Coping Strategies

Deconstruction of Identity

One of the biggest risk factors for a Native child is the destruction of their Native identity. According to the Swinomish Tribal Mental Health Project (1991), "Personal identity is tied to cultural identity" (p. 104). Psychologically, the systems and institutions that continually repeat the message that there is something wrong with everything about who you are, your family structure, your ancestry, your spirituality, your values and beliefs, and your socioeconomic status, leaves one to experience defeat, hopelessness, and powerlessness. The combination of these factors may be the concept Goodkind et al. (2015) referred to that O'Nell (1996) introduced: socially produced demoralization. The direct and peripheral messages from the media further affirm contradictory messages (explored further in chapter 6): success comes through hard work, but Natives are lazy; value yourself but your culture is insignificant (Swinomish Tribal Mental Health Project, 1991).

Hopelessness and Powerlessness

In thoroughly examining the factors that contribute to the Native child's identity, when all the factors are in question by a society that is not accepting of the child's identity, how would one not feel hopeless? How does this not lead to suicidality? In Johnston-Goodstar and VeLure Roholt's study (2017) about Native youth being pushed out of school, one of the interviewees, a Native youth caseworker, asked, "Are we killing them inside . . . ?" (p. 35) as it pertained to Native student's school experiences. Suicidal attempts may result from a desire to claim power in situations where the adolescent feels powerless.

Current statistics on suicidality in AI/AN youth report that their rate of suicide is the highest of any other demographic in the United States at a rate of 2.5 times greater than other races/ethnicities (NCAI, 2021b). As a humanitarian society, we should learn lessons from the past, as there are accounts from the boarding school era wherein Native students, stripped of their homeland, culture, family, and identity, willed themselves to death.

Substance Use

Although research on substance use by the AI/AN population is conflicted (Ross et al., 2020), the literature now includes positive outcome reports and no longer only portrays negative research and articles. The *drunken* Indian stereotype persists. However, research indicates the rates of abstinence from alcohol are highest among Native Americans as compared to other ethnic groups (Cunningham et al., 2016). Three recent studies conducted with college students also found that alcohol use by AI students was lower than their Caucasian counterparts in the upper Midwest (Martell et al., 2020; Sargent, 2017, 2020) and in the Southwest (Greenfield et al., 2018). Contextualizing the experiences of Native Americans within the frame of colonization and historical trauma allows for a more complex understanding of the impact of substance use, as it has been found to be dually colonialistic and remonstrative to colonialism (Matamonasa-Bennett, 2017).

Additional research has found that a greater percentage of Native Americans actively seek services for substance abuse than the general U.S. population, particularly when traditional healing and 12-step programs were included (Beals et al., 2006). Use of other substances including methamphetamine and opioids are present in Native communities and more research must be conducted in Native communities for accurate rates of affliction and impact. Regarding illicit substance use, Martell et al. (2020) and Sargent's study (2020) yielded similar rates of use between a Native and Caucasian college population. This was consistent with findings by Fish et al. (2017).

Older literature on substance use depicted a despairingly bleak outlook for the AI/AN population as documented in reports that Native Americans were found to be impacted by substances at younger ages and at higher rates than all other ethnic groups (Beals et al., 2005). Extensive alcohol consumption was reported to be a leading preventable cause of death in the United States and had considerable public health implications for Native people (May 1995; Mokdad et al., 2004). Earlier research also indicated that alcohol-attributable deaths (AAD) accounted for 11.7 percent of all AI/AN deaths, that the age-adjusted AAD rate for AI/ANs was approximately twice that of U.S. general population, and that AI/ANs lose 6.4 more years of potential life per AAD compared with persons in the U.S. general population (36.3 versus 29.9 years) (May 1995).

Traditional Native ways of life, practice of "culture," and re-traditionalism have been identified as mitigating factors for substance use with multiple Native populations (Hodge & Limb, 2010; Matamonasa-Bennett, 2017; Wolsko et al., 2007). These types of studies are important in balancing the Native narrative, unlike studies such as the Barrow Alcohol Study in the 1980s, which basically disenfranchised the entire Native population. Likely, more research conducted with the Native population by researchers using a cultural humility approach, and using community based participatory research models will result in the literature further shifting to a more accurate and balanced current day representation of substance use in Native communities.

Adverse Childhood Experiences

In terms of treatment challenges, the afore-referenced life circumstances, including broader racial discrimination and microaggressions, can contribute and exacerbate health disparities and inequities for the Native child and family (Goodkind et al., 2015; Moorehead et al., 2015; Ross, 2020; Suina, 2017; Walls et al., 2015), thereby increasing risk factors. ACEs are used as a mechanism to define Native children in psychological, psychiatric, educational, and judicial systems. The study of ACEs was initiated in 1998 by Felitti and colleagues, through use of a 17-question survey disseminated to patients of Kaiser Permanente's San Diego Health Appraisal Clinic. There was a 70.5 percent response rate. The participants were primarily middle class, approximately half were college graduates, 52 percent were women, and 80 percent were white. The participants in the original study were not representative of individuals residing in Indian Country.

Today, there are multiple forms and versions of the ACE survey that behavioral health departments and government agencies use to survey individuals. The ACE survey is routinely mandated to be used in behavioral health departments and medical facilities as a routine screening tool. Differences in these routine ACE surveys administered upon entry into a hospital or enrollment into behavioral health services are apparent when one department may use the original screener, another state may use a survey querying about occurrences in their lifetime, and the questions in the surveys may be completely different with additions, deletions, or variations of questions. Thus, when conclusions about ACEs are surmised related to the AI/AN population, one must ask if the comparisons to ACEs to other populations are based in the same operational definitions. Further, the assessor must assure the ACE surveys are congruent in composition so as not to skew data, results, and outcomes. One question on the survey specifically asks about having to wear dirty clothes, alluding to neglect; however, many Native communities still do not have running water. Therefore, other pertinent circumstances exist contributing to affirming the answer for other reasons than neglect. The answer to that question, though, constitutes one point on the ACE survey. Much work remains to be done with regard to ACEs and the Native population for an accurate accounting of affliction and impact (Brockie et al., 2013). In addition, local norms must be established for any tool or instrument used with the Native population.

Brockie et al. (2013) postulated that racism and symptoms related to historical loss, in combination with ACEs, modify epigenetics and increase the risk for health disparities and psychiatric disorder development in Native children, including an increased risk of suicide. Warne and Lajimodiere (2015) further discussed the need for scientific study of epigenetic modifications as a result of boarding school experiences and historical trauma in the context of ACEs. They expanded the dialogue about ACEs, illuminating relationships between these factors that contribute to chronic disease disparities across the lifespan, including the distribution of government program Women, Infants, and Children (WIC)—high rates of formula feeding of infants and Food Distribution Program on Indian Reservations (FDPIR)—high-calorie, low nutritional value foods in earlier program models. The Association of American Indian Physicians (2021) stated, "It seems likely that indigenous people experience unique ACEs that may include boarding school experiences, historical trauma from loss of land, culture, and language, as well as community-specific experiences" (para. 7). Based upon these Native expert's perspectives and knowledge, advocating for more studies pertaining specifically to the AI/AN population and ACEs is warranted, especially in light of routine assumptions made about Native Peoples with high ACE scores.

As an additional consideration related to stigma, racism, and oppression experienced by Native children, Walls et al. (2015) stated, "Psychosocial stress can adversely affect health in two major ways: directly, through neurochemical pathways; and indirectly, by promoting unhealthy behaviors" (p. 232). Blume et al. (2019) furthered the dialogue of discrimination and prejudice experienced by Native youth and the detrimental correlation with psychosocial functioning. Without an understanding of these factors related to the sociohistory of the Native child and family, the challenges to service delivery increases as the professional, educator, service provider, or practitioner's capability of relating to the individual they are serving lessens.

As alluded to earlier, treatment based in culturally competent, culturally relevant, cultural humility approaches, and traditional medicine are obstacles to effective treatment for Native patients. Traditional practices that contribute to health and well-being are unacknowledged by service providers (Bigfoot & Schmidt, 2012) and medicinal systems based in Indigenous knowledge continue to take a back seat in contemporary healing (Redvers & Blondin, 2020). Pomerville et al. (2016) stated "that Indigenous therapeutic approaches (such as traditional healing) should be accorded legitimacy in clinical contexts despite the lack of scientifically controlled outcome research" (p. 12). Native clients seeking treatment are also burdened with grossly negligent service previously provided, overpathologization by providers, and clinical racism. Duran and Duran (1995) asserted:

> One of the most important factors in the failure of the mental health delivery system is an inability of therapists to provide relevant forms of treatment to ethnic populations. . . . Most providers are trained only in delivering services to the majority/dominant population. Usually, therapists are completely unaware of the life experiences of the ethnic minority patient. (p. 8)

Enduring Courageousness

The strengths of Native children are bequeathed in their ancestry. Traditionally and contemporarily, Indigenous women take seriously the responsibility of not only caring for their own children, but all children. Although generations of systemic, institutional, governmental, and educational entities have sought to dismantle and destroy the essence of life for Native Peoples, the strength and courage of the People has endured. Mr. Regis Pecos expressed, "We're being forced to the very edge" with regard to where we are as a People. Therefore, we must push "somewhere back to the middle to a position where it's healthy, strong, and vibrant..." (personal communication, September 30, 2020). This strength and courageousness have taken on different forms since contact, thus the contemporary response to the welfare of Native children is embedded in the reclaiming and implementation of Native traditionalism and values without the interference of others. This counters the philosophy that Native Peoples do not know how to take care of their children.

Words of encouragement from Native elders have been an important aspect of Native history and culture. In the book *Our Stories, Our Lives,* twenty-three stories of Alaska Native elders, as told by themselves, are captured and recorded. One of the elders, Mr. Francis "Frank" Haldane, Tsimshian, spoke of some of his experiences growing up Alaska Native, serving in the military, and eventually retiring from the Federal Aviation Administration after thirty-five years of service. He offered this advice to Native youth:

> Be proud of self. Accept self for what you are, in spite of the conditions, in spite of your feelings. To accept self for what you are. To realize you are as good as anybody else that ever walked the face of the earth. That you have as much potential as anybody else anywhere. Although perhaps there's a lot of obstacles—big and small—along the way. (p. 154)

Mr. Haldane's words reinforce the guidance spoken by countless elders across the United States to Native children as they navigate life in two distinct cultural worlds. In some cases, for the protection and safety of Native children, these words have been used as counsel with adults as they have sought to dispute and challenge established U.S. laws and policies that have resulted in positioning Native children in high-risk classifications and in the detrimental outcomes of the Native child.

4

Current Policies and Laws Impacting Native Children, Adolescents, and Women

One of our challenges when we're trying to promote equity is that we also need to understand the truth. . . . The reason we have to understand these things is that if we are ever going to get to equity we have to walk through truth. Even when it's unpleasant. Even when it makes us uncomfortable . . . this is the truth of our history. And if we're going to get to the truth of the solutions, we better have a common understanding of the reality that our People face.

—Donald Warne, Oglala Lakota, MD, MPH (2019); UND associate dean of Diversity, Equity, and Inclusion; INMED director

Child maltreatment in the American Indian/Alaska Native (AI/AN) population assumes many inconceivable forms covered in this chapter. Although these conditions exist, the Native poulation continues to persevere and seek justice in a myriad of ways, including litigation, lobbying, policy making, activism, allyship, collaboration, traditional practices, and prayer. Restoration of balance and societal equity for Native People can be achieved through courageous conversations, recognition and acknowledgement of societal ills in Indian Country, reparation of historical transgressions, and durable, enforceable laws and policies that provide comprehensive protection for Native children, women, and families.

Status

Overall, the AI/AN population experiences more interracial violence than other races (Gordon & Roberts, 2021; Rosay, 2021). Thus, violence perpetrated upon Native Peoples is committed by other than AI/AN persons. In addition, compared to other races, Native People "had the highest victimization rates for both women and men and across all ages, locations (urban, suburban, and rural), and household incomes" (p. 94), especially as it pertains to assaults (sexual, aggravated, and simple) and rape (Rosay, 2021). Governmental laws and policies have not protected children born of AI/AN heritage in the United States. There are many loopholes within judicial and law enforcement systems that significantly relinquish protection of the safety and welfare of Native Peoples. Newly appointed U.S. Interior Secretary Debra Haaland stated, "Violence against Indigenous peoples is a crisis that has been underfunded for decades. Far too often, murders and missing persons cases in Indian country go unsolved and unaddressed, leaving families and communities devastated" (Balsamo & Samuels, 2021). The lack of federal and state prosecution of crimes committed against Native children and adults has also been a tremendous source of frustration for Native victims and tribes (Deer, 2017).

Protection and Safety

Generally, the protections afforded a child under the age of eighteen, per definition of tribal, state, and federal laws, should begin and rest comfortably with safeguards designated by the parent and/or guardian and the laws set forth in that domain. Conventionally, that simple point is customary in the dominant society and consideration of any other potential parental circumstances does not resonate. For Native children, existing contemporary laws and policies in tribal communities are a maze of navigation for their protection and safety, whether the child resides within the exterior boundaries of U.S. tribal lands or those who reside off reservation. These laws and policies, constantly in negotiation from several centuries ago into the world of today, have implications in tribal, state, and federal arenas and affect the estimated 574,313 AI/AN families in 2017 in the United States (National Congress of American Indians [NCAI], 2021b).

Contemporary Circumstances

Social order. Principles necessitating order in Native communities have always been in existence (LaFortune & Rush, 2019). In AI/AN populations, rules of social order and laws were advocated orally and modeled by tribal elders, parents, and leaders. Outsiders from foreign nations, encountering Native populations during the contact period, did not acknowledge these tribal principles, laws, and rules, and their perception was that law and order among the tribal communities were lacking or had not been established, and lawlessness was rampant. These misperceptions and misinterpretations of tribal community dynamics were derived from a European concept of law that grievously differed from concepts of tribal law and order. The practice of societal laws in tribal communities were not written; they were practiced from within a collectivistic orientation, and the rules for order were ingrained in the community. In some tribes, an annual recitation of governing laws was announced at ceremonial events (LaFortune & Rush, 2019).

In pondering the construct of "lawlessness," one must examine how these sizeable societies of people could survive for millenniums without order being existent. Various accounts of the estimated Native population in the Americas include numbers as high as twenty million before European contact, with approximately five million in the U.S. territory (Warne, 2019). Tribes numbered in the range of 600 (Crofoot Graham, 2002). Due to the attempted genocide of the

Native U.S. population through various forces (see chapter 2), in or about 1900 the Native U.S. population was reduced to less than 200,000 (Warne, 2019). Today, 3.7 million people singularly identify as AI/AN and an additional 5.9 million people identify themselves as being AI/AN in combination with another race (NCAI Policy Research Center, 2021). The United States federally recognizes 574 tribes, located in thirty-five states. "Once a federal reservation is established, only Congress can diminish or disestablish it. Doing so requires a clear expression of congressional intent" (Supreme Court of the United States, 2020).

Today, little is commonly known about the Indigenous Peoples of the United States, as documented in a project where 13,000 Americans were surveyed in 2016. "For example, many respondents believe(d) there aren't many Native Americans left in America and report(ed) not knowing any native people. Presumably, that ignorance extends to knowledge of native court systems as well" (LaFortune & Rush, 2019, para. 1). Thus, many of the issues presented in this book may conceivably be the first time individuals may have encountered historical or contemporary information about the AI/AN population and very likely be the first time the issues facing Native children and families have been contextualized from an Indigenous worldview.

Laws. The laws created, enacted, and enforced in Indian Country were not created by Native Peoples (G. Vigil, personal communication December 11, 2020). The laws to which Native Peoples were subjected and to which they adhered, were forced on them by various governments within the United States, without recourse, and were incompatible with traditional law. "When we're not in control . . . the impact to our way of thinking and how we feel is profoundly diminished. It's like the incompatibility of traditional peacemaking or restorative justice" as compared to western prosecutorial systems (R. Pecos, personal communication September 30, 2020). Within a traditional structure, "Historically, tribes exercised sovereignty in full, including addressing threats to children's safety and wellbeing . . . Tribal elders acted as judges. Traditional chiefs governed as the protectors of family well-being. Tribal clan and kinship systems functioned as social service providers" (Simmons, 2014, p. 4). Mr. R. Pecos, a traditionalist, scholar, and state legislative senior policy advisor, asserted traditional justice doctrines are an Indigenous knowledge system obscured within a western framework (personal communication, September 30, 2020) and are not incorporated in a western judicial system.

The federal government has a responsibility to provide medical, educational (Brayboy & Chin, 2020), and law enforcement services, negotiated through U.S. treaties, unless the tribal entity has opted to take over the services, via Public Law 93–638 regulations and compliance. One might infer from all the historical trauma the Native population has endured that the laws created with respect to the Native population have not been for the purpose of safety and protection. For example, as noted in chapter 3, Native children have been targeted for removal and adoption at greater rates than any other population in the United States. As previously iterated, Native children continue to be at risk for removal and foster care placement at a rate four times greater than dominant society children (NICWA, 2021).

Some of the contemporary issues related to the overall welfare of Native children are related to sovereignty, jurisdictional issues, prosecutorial declinations, and negligible response to important issues facing AI/AN families and children. In the recent past, many tribes have brought awareness to the dismal rates of prosecution, hence declination rates by the U.S. Attorney offices in Indian Country. According to Kastelic (2013), the Transactional Records Access Clearinghouse at Syracuse University compiled data indicating prosecutors declined 52 percent of cases involving serious crimes in Indian Country. Deer (2017) reported a 2010 U.S. Government Accountability Office report documented federal prosecutors' declination rates of sexual abuse and related matters at 67 percent between the years of 2005–2009, which means these child victims and their families never saw any justice and the offenders had no accountability for their crimes. Layers of complications plague prosecution, including inconsistencies in investigatory procedures, lack of jurisdictional coordination, opaque operational definitions of child abuse and neglect (Kastelic, 2013), problems practical, legal, factual, or logistical (EchoHawk, 2001), and evidentiary complications (Deer, 2017). Thus, many offenders in criminal cases have benefitted from legal loopholes, but the systemic siloing of entities responsible for the protection of child victims not working together is a larger issue.

In many venues, it has been proposed that the lack of response by law enforcement and jurisdictional loophole circumstances have contributed greatly to missing and murdered Native people for decades (Ross et al., 2018). Due to these same loopholes, Native children are prime targets for victimization, which also contributes to the rates of victimization as stated at the beginning of the chapter. Seeking justice for Native Peoples in remote, rural, and urban tribal communities has continued judicial, systemic, and institutional challenges.

Jurisdictional Maze. Today, there are an estimated 400 tribal justice court systems in the United States (Bureau of Indian Affairs, n.d.). In Indian Country, the maze of federal Indian policy creates judicial nightmares for children and families. Though a comprehensive review of American Indian sovereignty law and policy is beyond the scope of this book, here is a brief overview. In the most basic terms, tribal lands are sovereign nations and have a government-to-government relationship with the United States. These terms were negotiated through U.S. treaties during the overtaking of tribal lands. Generally, children enrolled in a federally recognized U.S. tribe living on tribal lands are under the purview of tribal law and order codes with federal supervision responsibility. NCAI (2021) reported tribal judicial systems are present in about 59 percent of tribes. In some cases, traditional law continues to pervade judicial affairs; other tribes utilize a blended justice system combining traditional and western aspects; and some tribes have elected to develop and implement specific laws pertaining to children, identified as "children's codes." In one tribe's children's code, the right to be treated with dignity is addressed, wherein reintegration and a constructive role in the community are important goals and outcomes (Pueblo of Laguna, 2020). The Children's Code purpose states that the tribal council "recognize that the future of our existence as a people is intricately connected to the safety and welfare of all children . . . (and) enacts this chapter to establish policies and procedures to protect the interests of its children, families, the (community) and its customs and traditions, laws and culture" (Pueblo of Laguna, 2020, Section 7-1-1, para. 1).

In resolving crimes committed against a child, the appropriate prosecutorial jurisdictional venue of the offender must first be determined based upon the offender's race. This determination of venue will also dictate the tribal, state, or federal mental health treatment services to which the child victim may be entitled and may reside in concurrent entities. The prosecution of crimes involving Native children on and off tribal lands has many nuances in prosecutorial realms and varies greatly, due to the many challenges of federal, state, and tribal law. In general, when a crime occurs against a Native American child on federally recognized tribal lands and the perpetrator is Native, if the crime is a misdemeanor, it is subsequently prosecuted in tribal court. If the crime meets felonious criteria and considered part of the Major Crimes Act (18 U.S.C.A. 1153), passed in 1885 by Congress, the federal government has criminal jurisdiction and the Federal Bureau of Investigation (FBI) retains the responsibility for investigation. These crimes, felony child abuse or neglect, sexual abuse of a minor, kidnapping, murder, rape, manslaughter, and incest, are then prosecuted in the federal court system. Many crimes committed against Native American children on tribal lands meet criteria for federal prosecution and it is possible for a person to be charged concurrently in tribal and federal court, which does not pose double jeopardy status. In addition, if federal prosecution is declined, the case may be referred back to the tribal court system for prosecution if the offender is Native. An exception exists if the offender is non-Native, as tribal courts do not have any jurisdiction over the offender. Thus, if federal prosecution is declined for a case involving a Native victim(s) of child abuse or child sexual abuse committed by a non-Native, the offender eludes culpability and any legal consequences.

In some states, the state retains jurisdiction over Native American tribes, and criminal offenses are subject to state prosecution and adjudication. These states are known as PL83–280 states, and include California, Minnesota, Nebraska, Oregon, Wisconsin, and Alaska. In Montana, one reservation is subject to PL83–280 for prosecution of felony crimes. In August 1953, Congress enacted Public Law 280, which authorized those states to assume responsibility for civil and criminal jurisdiction over those tribes located in their respective areas.

Missing Native Peoples

Throughout the history of the United States, Native Peoples across the lifespan have resoundingly been the subject of victimization in criminal, political, educational, judicial, and medical arenas, to name a few. With regard to victimization of Native females, Deer (2019) asserted, "The rates of violence are an extension of the historical mistreatment and dehumanization of Native women" (p. 3). These horrendous abuses extend to children and constitute child maltreatment.

Missing and Murdered Indigenous Women and Girls

Prosecution of domestic violence and interpersonal violent crimes has been an ongoing problem in Indian Country, which has contributed to perpetuation of these crimes, and in some cases resulted in death. Deer (2017) stated, "the United States (is) a culpable bystander in the high rates of sexual violence perpetrated against Native women and children, which developed over time due to policies of official indifference . . . and for allowing this dynamic to remain unabated for hundreds of years" (p. 772). According to the NCAI (2021), the rate of assault (homicide) on the AI/AN population is 11.4 percent in comparison to 5.4 percent for all other races—more than double the rate for other ethnic groups. In 2017, Montana Senator Steve Daines attested between the ages of ten and twenty-four, the third leading cause of death among AI/AN girls and women was homicide. Grassroots efforts initiated by family members in or about 2015 who have lost sisters, daughters, aunties, grandmothers, nieces initially brought awareness to the Missing and Murdered Indigenous Women and Girls (MMIWG) movement, which included early adolescent and teenage girls. In concert with the grassroots efforts of many AI/AN individuals, the Society of Indian Psychologists authored a white paper (Ross et al., 2018) calling for the closing of jurisdictional loopholes with which many non-Native men are familiar.

These loopholes increase the likelihood that Native women and girls are targeted for violence as the enforcement of the law in Indian Country with non-Native perpetrators continues to present a complex web of jurisdictional labyrinths. Rosay (2016) conducted a study that yielded the following: of the Native women reporting victimization, 96 percent reported at least one instance of sexual violence perpetrated upon them was committed by a non-Native offender. Further compounding their victimization, the laws in Indian Country are remiss around stalking and other attendant crimes, thus reducing protections for AI/AN women and children (Ross et al., 2018). In the study by Rosay (2016), 49 percent of Native women who made reports said they experienced stalking and 66 percent had experienced psychological violence. Protections for these Native women and girls are further weakened by the status of public safety in Indian Country—for every 1,000 tribal residents, there are only 1.3 sworn police officers, based on a 2008 report (NCAI, 2021), and these law enforcement officers are responsible for policing an area totaling 49,933 square miles.

Specific environmental factors related to economic ventures, including oil booms and mining located near tribal reservations, have increased the rate of violence against Native American women and girls, as these industries bring more non-Native men into the area. In consideration of all these aforementioned circumstances, federal, state, and local entities can cite the number of missing or murdered women in their respective jurisdictions. However, the accuracy of the data related to MMIWG remains unknown as a dearth of statistical information exists regarding these persons. The reasons alluded to for these conditions were in part attributed to systemic and institutional racism, various jurisdictional conflicts, and Native women were categorized as "Other" when race was reported (Ross et al., 2018). Initially, the issue of MMIWG and Missing and Murdered Indigenous People (MMIP) was brought to the attention of the public through grassroots efforts by families and tribal community members affected by these tragedies. In addition, efforts modeled effectively by our neighbors to the north in Canada, such as the Canadian government initiating a National Inquiry into Missing and Murdered Indigenous Women and Girls in 2016 and lawful inquiry efforts by Dr. Beverly Jacobs and others helped to ignite the furor and injustice experienced by AI/AN families in the United States.

According to Trent Shores, U.S. Attorney in the Northern District of Oklahoma, in his May 21, 2020, address to the President's Commission on Law Enforcement and the Administration of Justice, "It is extremely difficult to develop a cure for a problem when its scope is unknown. The United States must continue to lead by example to promote and protect the inherent rights of indigenous people" (Shores, 2020, para. 23). As a society, we must continue to support legislation and efforts to strengthen laws that protect women and children from violence and victimization, such as Savanna's Act (2020) and the Not Invisible Act (2019), passed by Congress. The National Missing and Unidentified Persons System (NamUs) has finally begun to collaborate with Native families and tribal nations to enter demographics and other related information on MMIP. Seven offices were opened across the country to specifically address MMIP, including cold case investigations into MMIP. The Department of Justice's Operation Lady Justice Task Force has begun training sessions for public and law enforcement entities related to information on MMIP collected over a one-year period. In order to develop clear directives for addressing MMIWG through specific legislation, policies, and enforcement, we must make a concerted effort to fully explore the thorough impact of this crisis in Native communities. Shining the light on the underreporting of missing Native children, in any capacity, remains a critical concern in Indian Country.

Missing Native Children

The actual numbers of missing U.S. Indigenous children are unknown. In 2016, there were 7,700 reported Native youth missing according to the AMBER Alerts in Indian Country fact sheet (Office of Juvenile Justice and Delinquency Prevention [OJJDP], 2017). This number is estimated to be higher but reflects that 1 in 130 Native American children likely goes missing each year (OJJDP, 2017). The National Center for Missing & Exploited Children (NCMEC) documented 1,909 reports of missing Native children between the period of January 1, 2009, to December 31, 2018 (Clark, 2021). The mean age of those missing Native children was eleven years old. Most of them lived off tribal lands, 70 percent were missing from alternative residential locations (e.g., group homes and foster care), however, 162 were children missing from tribal "territory" (Clark, 2021). Inconsistent support and advocacy leave many Native families feeling anxious and without answers about their lost children and relatives. Remedying the reporting system will provide additional insight into this problematic issue.

Prior to 2018, there was no system in place to provide assistance to Native families whose child or children went missing. Thus, if a child was kidnapped, lost, or stolen, there were few resources available for finding the missing child. Incredulously, before 2018, the AMBER Alert system had not been available to tribal law enforcement in reservation communities to make mass notifications for a missing Native child/children. Unfortunately, many Native children died as a result of this deficiency for the protection of Native American children. The systematic oppression inherent within the reporting system and response contributed to devaluing children of color, specifically Indigenous children, to the point of not being inclusive in reporting or facilitating a unified response effort for these children.

The brutal murder of eleven-year-old Ashlynne Mike in May 2016, initially reported as a missing child after she did not return home from school, set the stage for proposed national legislation, as the AMBER Alert system was still not in place in Indian Country. Ashlynne Mike's abduction was not broadcasted via an AMBER Alert until the following morning at 2:30 a.m. (Walters & Blasing, 2021), but she had already been violently assaulted and killed. Finally, in 2018, the U.S. Senate made modifications to expand the missing-child alert systems to American Indian reservations via a bill introduced by Senator John McCain (Ashlynne Mike, 2018). On March 22, 2018, in the 115th U.S. Congress, the Senate approved the Ashlynne Mike AMBER Alert in Indian Country Act (Congress .gov, 2018). The passing of this Act provides parity in tribes having direct access to AMBER Alert infrastructure funding for tribal accessibility and was signed into law on April 13, 2018. Currently, about one hundred tribes in thirty-four states are building infrastructure and making progress toward connecting to the AMBER Alert system (Clark, 2021). Our nation must demand provisions of 34 U.S. Code §41307, Reporting requirement for missing children, and 34 U.S. Code § 41308, State requirements for reporting missing children, (uscode.house.gov, n.d.) be followed when any Native child is reported missing.

The implementation of the AMBER Alert in Indian Country affords U.S. tribes equitable law enforcement response notification that the rest of the country has had instituted for decades when a Native child goes missing. Recently, in September 2018, a missing Native child was reported in a region of northwestern Alaska and a massive search ensued. Hopefully, this child's death will not be in vain, as this was one of the first cases involving an Indigenous child where a large contingency of federal, state, and local entities contributed their resources to locating this child, including approximately seventeen members of the FBI.

Laws must continue to be strengthened and enforced for the protection of Native children who have been murdered or missing, abused, or otherwise violated psychologically, emotionally, physically, and those who have been truly neglected. Additionally, policies addressing culturally informed and trauma-informed approaches when serving Native children and their families will facilitate more connection with Native communities. Exploring laws, policies, and practice-based evidence that begin to embrace some of the aforementioned approaches of working with Native communities will follow in chapters 5 and 6.

Indian Child Welfare Act of 1978

Laws protecting U.S. Native American children and families have been insufficient to protect them from separation. As discussed in chapter 2, removal of Native children from their families and tribes can be traced back to government and church institutions with a focus to assimilate Native children into the dominant culture. Some of the assimilative methods used were accomplished through orphanage placement, educational institutional placement, and private adoptions. Lomawaima (2018) argues that in "before and after" images of Native youth attending boarding schools, the "before" photos where the children were in Native regalia were taken with darkened lenses, and the images were subsequently lightened in the "after" pictures where the children were in western uniforms. This propaganda was designed to send a message to Native parents, "We can take better care of your children than you can" (p. 17). However, more realistic unretouched pictures exist of children attending boarding schools in which their clothes are dirty and tattered, hair mussed, and barefoot, which depicts the true status of attendees at these institutes of learning (Lomawaima, 2018).

Indian Adoption Act

The Indian Adoption Act, in place from 1959 to 1967, was instituted through a joint effort between the Bureau of Indian Affairs, the

U.S. Children's Bureau, and the Child Welfare League of America (Palmiste, 2011). The set rules for non-Native adoption were initially tested with fifty Native children, who were at least one-fourth degree of consanguinity, emotionally and physically adoptable, and "after good counselling" (p. 3) were released by the parent (Palmiste, 2011). The intent of the project was to increase the desirability of Native children for white middle class family adoption (Crofoot & Harris, 2012). Between 1961 and 1976, the estimated number of adopted Native children was totaled at 12,486 (Palmiste, 2011). However, the numbers of adoptions may be underreported, as they are based on the accuracy of reporting parties whose motivation, in part, was cultural genocide.

Indian Child Welfare Act of 1978. The Indian Child Welfare Act (ICWA) of 1978 was a federal law enacted to end illegal adoptions and place "Indian children" with Native families. Crofoot & Harris (2012) established that an "Indian child" was defined as "any unmarried person who is under age eighteen and is either (a) a member of an Indian tribe or (b) is eligible for membership in an Indian tribe and is the biological child of a member of an Indian tribe" (925 USC 1606, p. 1667). Although improvements have been made, NICWA (2021) reported AI/AN families are four times more likely to have their children removed and placed in the child welfare system than their white peers. NICWA (2015) made the following statement regarding Native adoptions, "Until ICWA is followed, AI/AN children and families will continue to face discrimination in the child welfare system, will continue to be removed at alarming rates, and will continue to be placed in risky adoptions" (para. 1). Regarding Native children whose adoptions were guided by ICWA guidelines, these children fared equitable or better than state care non-Indian adopted children (Limb et al., 2004; Society of Indian Psychologists [SIP], 2015).

ICWA has been ignored, unenforced, and challenged since the law was passed in 1978. In recent history, the law was challenged in 2013 stemming from class action litigation in the Federal district court in the District of Arizona filed by the Goldwater Institute who claimed ICWA violated the Constitution regarding adoptions of Native children in *A.D. v. Washburn.* The case was ultimately dismissed. In 2018, ICWA was again challenged and ruled unconstitutional by a federal judge in the Northern District of Texas in *Brackeen v. Bernhard*. According to the presiding judge, ICWA was discriminatory to the adoption of Native children by non-Native prospective parents and secondly, the judge determined ICWA federal statutes directed states to adhere to the lawful tenets of the U.S. government. Attorneys appealed the ruling, and a stay had been issued by the U.S. Fifth Circuit Court of Appeals. In August 2019, ICWA was upheld. The Court's opinion on *Brackeen v. Bernhard* (2019) included the following:

> For these reasons, we conclude that Plaintiffs had standing to bring all claims and that ICWA and the Final Rule are constitutional because they are based on a political classification that is rationally related to the fulfillment of Congress's unique obligation toward Indians; ICWA preempts conflicting state laws and does not violate the Tenth Amendment anticommandeering doctrine; and ICWA and the Final Rule do not violate the nondelegation doctrine. We also conclude that the Final Rule implementing the ICWA is valid because the ICWA is constitutional, the BIA did not exceed its authority when it issued the Final Rule, and the agency's interpretation of ICWA section 1915 is reasonable. (p. 46)

Currently, several states have begun the process of codifying federal ICWA law into state law (NICWA, 2021) including New Mexico, with the 2022 New Mexico Legislature passing the HB-135 Indian Family Protection Act, and signed by the govenor. Other states are currently collaborating to develop policies that support child welfare reform, and they are being reexamined with culturally informed stakeholders. Legislators, state leadership, law enforcement, state social service departments, and federal entities must support and honor the Indian Child Welfare Act for the protection and safety of Native children. Laws that support child welfare must also be reexamined and reformed.

Medical Systems: Reproduction, Sterilization, and Sexual Abuse

The use of traditional healing systems is preferred by many Indigenous Peoples. Some tribal members avoid western medical health care providers and systems altogether. Negative feelings associated with hospitals and predicated on unconceivable circumstances are based in maltreatment. The laws pertaining to the medical health of the AI/AN population, as with any other population, should be protected by those who enact laws and policies and by those performing the services serving the AI/AN population that take an oath to do no harm. The laws and policies that govern the care of Native Peoples need to be strengthened, and accountability must be elevated. Native People are afflicted by health disparities at a higher rate than other populations in the United States (NCAI, 2021; Ross et al., 2020; Walls et al., 2015; Warne, 2019). These disparities exist in both tribal lands and urban areas where Native children reside. The current life expectancy for the AI/AN population is 5.5 years less in comparison to other populations in the United States (NCAI, 2021).

Promise of Medical Care

Medical Systems. Medical care was promised in perpetuity by the U.S. government in exchange for the ceding of tribal lands and by law throughout the colonizing of the United States (Brayboy & Chin, 2020). The Indian Health Service (IHS), under the umbrella of the U.S. Department of Health and Human Services, provides obligatory direct medical and public health services; it was originally established under the U.S. Department of War. Today, services are provided to members of federally recognized AI/AN tribal members. McDonald et al. (1993) documented IHS facilities were "typically overworked, understaffed, underfunded, and have long waiting lists" (p. 446). Those conditions remain the same in 2022 and were glaringly illuminated in the COVID-19 pandemic.

In 2017, healthcare funding comparisons are as follow: per capita, the United States allocated $9,726 for National Health spending, $10,692 per Veterans Medical patient, $8,109 per Medicaid enrollee, and $4,078 for IHS users (Warne, 2021). Francys Crevier, Chief Executive Officer, National Council of Urban Indian Health, offered testimony at the United Nations Virtual Consultation—Situation of Indigenous Peoples Living in Urban Areas on March 17, 2021, that $672 was allocated for urban Indian patients for healthcare *per year.* Thus, the disparity in funding for IHS trickles down to the availability of resources for treatment of the AI/AN population. Though some in dominant society are upset the AI/AN population receives "free" healthcare, these individuals assume quality care is provided and do not understand the outcomes and health status disparities in the AI/AN populations (Ross et al., 2020). Many tribal nation IHS facilities have a history of negligence, as presented in the few instances that follow. Of note, the death rate for the AI/AN population is higher than any other U.S. population as a result of overall "chronic illness including diabetes, chronic liver disease, cirrhosis, mellitus, and suicide" (NCAI, 2021b, para. 7).

Sterilization. Based in eugenical rationale, although relatively unknown and not eagerly disclosed in U.S. history, Native women and girls were involuntarily sterilized as early as the 1950s through the mid-1970s at the behest of IHS doctors employed by the U.S. government (Lawrence, 2000; Luker, 2000; U.S. Government Accountability Office [GAO], 1976). The full accounting of AI/AN women sterilized remains unknown, as a full GAO investigation was not conducted (Luker, 2000). Native women seeking medical care for various medical maladies were unknowingly sterilized and, in many of these cases, no consent was obtained. There are countless stories originating in different parts of Indian Country from women and girls about the circumstances of their sterilization. For example, in an upper Midwest Indian Health Service hospital, two fifteen-year-old girls went in for appendectomy surgery. In addition to their surgery, they were sterilized without their consent, nor was consent obtained from their parents (Lawrence, 2000). According to Luker (2000), reasons cited for forced sterilization included coerced, threatened, and misinformed consent; lack of consent or knowledge; and added sterilization in conjunction with other surgery.

This forced sterilization continued into 1976 and an estimated rate of sterilization was between 25 and 50 percent (Lawrence, 2000; Minthorn, 2018). After receiving numerous reported unauthorized accounts of sterilization, an investigation was conducted into the IHS. A Government Accountability Office (GAO) report (1976) stated that 3,406 Native women between the ages of fifteen to forty-four were sterilized between 1973 and 1976. Many were under the age of twenty-one and in comparison, those numbers would have been equivalent to 452,000 non-Native women in the same time period (Luker, 2000). This policy has had AI/AN population implications and underlies birth rates associated with Native women, as the birth rate reduced between the 1970 and 1980 U.S. census from 3.79 to 1.80 (Luker, 2000). According to the GAO report (1976), none of the women and girls involuntarily sterilized were interviewed, as it was deemed it would have been unproductive.

There has been an assertion by some in the dominant society that Native people should not reproduce as they are not "fit," consistent with Galton's eugenics movement (Luker, 2000). Another common insinuation was that Native People were incapable of caring for their children (Palmiste, 2011) or the parenting of their children was defective, inadequate, and flawed. Therefore, the sterilization of Native women was inconsequential based on this belief. There was no accountability for the medical personnel who implemented this atrocious medical practice (Luker, 2000). As observed by Minthorn (2018), this criminal sterilization of Native women has resulted in the decline of the Native population (the potential for these women to have children), depression (inability to get pregnant; childless women not by choice; unauthorized hysterectomies), and the overall systemic contribution to the attempted demise of the Native family (perpetuation of intergenerational trauma and deconstruction of Native families). In addition, sterilization resulted in "higher rates of marital problems, alcoholism, drug abuse, psychological . . . difficulties, shame, and guilt" (Lawrence, 1999, p. 80). Today, full IHS audits still have not been conducted and a tangible fear of this happening continues to exist for Native women (Luker, 2000). Given the recent scrutiny of unethical health care practices related to the U.S. Immigration and Customs Enforcement (ICE) engaging in unwanted and unnecessary hysterectomies of migrant detainees in a Georgia Detention Center (Rameriz, 2020), it appears that history may be repeating itself and a united call is in order to address our collective society, lawmakers, scholars, and professionals such that they demand equitable medical service delivery for the original Peoples of this country.

Molestation. Children, one of the most vulnerable populations in our modern society, have been sexually violated while they were patients at the Indian Health Service (IHS). On February 13, 2020, an IHS pediatrician was sentenced to five lifetime prison terms plus forty-five years for sexual abusing underage Native male patients while working in South Dakota and Montana (U.S. Department of Justice [USDOJ], 2021; Weaver & Frosch, 2020). The full accounting of this individual's victims remains unknown, since many victims of child sexual abuse do not report molestation for various reasons. The result of the molestation for some of the victims was drug use, arrests, incarceration, and a myriad of psychological trauma (Johnson et al, 2019).

Suspicions of this person's molestation of clients dated back to the 1990s; however, this individual was allowed to work steadily for decades, and only resigned in 2016 while under federal investigation (Chiedi, 2019). During the twenty-year period this since-convicted medical doctor worked for IHS, two Native psychologists, Daniel Foster and Rebecca Foster, among many others, reported their suspicions. The response from IHS was to transfer the pediatrician to other facilities. Special Agent Fred Bennett, Rosebud Sioux, Bureau of Indian Affairs, Office of Justice Services, working the Pine Ridge Reservation, finally successfully convinced a victim to record the abuse he endured, and this initiated investigative intercession (USDOJ, 2021). It should be noted that these Native providers were persistent in their reporting and supporting of victims, and that led to accountability for the crimes that were committed against community members. Trust among providers is essential and is clearly aligned with efforts to advocate within Native communities and protect Native children who seek services.

Other IHS reports of sexual abuse involving patients have surfaced and been filed throughout the years, with some victims under the age of eighteen. How many reports were not made, destroyed, or ignored? Undoubtedly, the individuals who were investigated, terminated, charged, and convicted have been in the minority, and unknown Native victims have been left to endure physical and psychological trauma over the lifespan. Fortunately, a federal task force, Protecting Native American Children in the IHS System, was initiated in March 2019 (Chiedi, 2019) and their findings were reported in 2020 (USDOJ, 2021). Reporting procedures and laws must be indisputably strengthened to protect Native children, as gaps in the law and uneven implementation of new policies continue to exist. Sen. John Hoeven (R, N.D.), chairman of the Senate Committee on Indian Affairs, stated IHS employee misconduct and patient abuse must be addressed (USDOJ, 2021). Law and policies that strengthen the safety and protection of Native children must be instituted and enforced.

Racial Profiling of Pregnant Native Women: COVID-19

In 2020, in response to the COVID-19 pandemic, some pregnant Native women were separated from their babies at birth based upon their zip code, which coincided with post office locales positioned in tribal lands. According to a *ProPublica* (Furlow, 2020) investigative news story, some pregnant Native mothers were administered COVID-19 tests without consent and some of those women whose COVID-19 results were still pending when they went into labor were separated from their newborns at birth. Hospital administrators ordered and implemented this racially discriminatory practice at a large metropolitan southwest hospital. This hospital allegedly claimed they based this practice on CDC guidelines. However, the isolation of the patients and the mother/child separation were related to the phenotype of the pregnant mother and the zip code in which she resided. The discrimination of these expectant Native women resulted in being treated differently because of their race/ethnicity, with negative implications for the critical bonding period with their babies, negative impacts to the mother's mental health due to the separation, and the potential impact for resultant attachment issues.

An official investigation of these incidents was initiated, and *ProPublica* reported not only were treatment protocol documents removed, but employees were discouraged from communicating with investigators from the state (Furlow, 2020). The findings were forwarded to the U.S. Department of Health and Human Services' Office for Civil Rights. The American Civil Liberties Union Reproductive Rights Attorney, Ellie Rushforth, made the following statement (excerpt):

These actions mirror the historic and violent practices of the U.S. government and medical systems deceiving and forcibly sterilizing Native American women, experimenting on Native communities without informed consent, and forcibly assimilating Native American children by removing them from their families and placing them in boarding schools, foster homes, and adoption systems. That Lovelace Hospital would continue this legacy of oppression and pretend it was for the best interest of patients is repugnant. Singling women and their babies out for discrimination based on race is not only unethical and abhorrent, it flies in the face of medical best practices, including informed consent and perinatal care. It also subjects Native American women, who are already at an increased risk of maternal morbidity and mortality as a result of systemic racism, to further harm. (2020, para. 3)

Research has found there are multiple bonding and attachment implications for separating mothers from their infants. The psychological impact of this practice will leave lasting effects on the mothers whose newly born infants were separated from them. When we contemplate the complex lived histories Natives endure in combination with intergenerational trauma, future studies examining the family attachment of individuals who have been separated from their children will be necessary to explore the long-term effects of early separation, particularly examining the additional stressors of the pandemic and sociopolitical unrest.

The previous two sections on missing Native persons and medical care are presented in part, to provide an awareness to the reader of current biopsychosocial child maltreatment related to Indigenous children. In order for equity and transformation to occur, awareness must become action, and consequently impact a massive shift in systems. Laws pertaining to consent for medical procedures must be applied equally to all those served. Advocacy and lobbying efforts must be egalitarian for all constituents and include parity for all ethnic populations.

Education Reform

The educational needs and concerns of Indigenous students have often been brought to the fore by Native students, parents, educators, and tribal nations. However, meaningful change in equity and educational standardization has not occurred or has moved at glacial speed. The current educational system for Native students has been deficient in meeting the educational needs of AI/AN students, although their education is mandated by federal, state, and local government entities.

Self-Determination
Around 1970, the U.S. government gave the tribes funding for self-governance programs in their tribal nations under the umbrella of self-determination. However, the tribes were also told how to establish

and operate their programs, which contradicted the doctrines of self-determination (G. Vigil, personal communication, March 24, 2021). Although these self-determination policies have retained federal oversight, this has been considered by some the only effective policy resulting in making significant progress toward the reversal of sociocultural and socioeconomic circumstances in tribal Native communities (Cornell & Kalt, 2010). In order for tribes to fully attain self-determination, self-governance program rules and policies must be liberated and sanction full control of operations by tribal entities, which has not been the case.

Equity in Education. After attempts to remedy negative results for inclusion and equity on behalf of Native children within the system of oversight failed, tribes have turned to litigation as a viable option. Brayboy offered the following with regard to laws about education:

> I'm not entirely convinced that the laws are insufficient. I think the way that they've been applied and taken up and interpreted are wholly insufficient. So, for me there are laws and policies on the book that call for self-determining education, they call for culturally responsive scoring, they call for self-determined schools, and for tribally driven schools. What ends up happening is people that make decisions don't actually enact those policies and laws as they were written. So maybe it's splitting hairs here, I think. Part of the problem with the laws in terms of them being insufficient is there does not appear to be sufficient enough teeth to hold people responsible for actually doing what the law says they're supposed to do. (Personal communication, March 10, 2021)

In part due to the insufficiency of the education of Native students, two recent lawsuits in southwest states were filed, litigated, and the outcomes are being implemented. These cases seek to compel educational entities to provide equitable educational opportunities to Native students.

In Arizona, *Stephen C. v. Bureau of Indian Education* (BIE), 3:17-cv-08004 was filed—a civil rights lawsuit related to Havasupai Elementary School students with disabilities (Public Counsel, 2020). The educational needs of Native students with disabilities were not being met. The school is remotely located at the bottom of the Grand Canyon. The historic lawsuit was settled on October 2, 2020, by

Arizona U.S. District Court Judge, Steven Logan. The main question in the lawsuit revolved around whether "school districts [are] required to provide disability services to children who've suffered trauma related to poverty and discrimination" (Washburn, 2018, para. 1). In Judge Logan's ruling, he stated that the plaintiffs had "adequately alleged that complex trauma and adversity can result in physiological effects constituting a physical impairment" (Washburn, 2018, para. 3). Judge Logan acknowledged the denial of educational opportunities for Native students with disabilities and remedied circumstances could have implications in the 183 other BIE schools across the nation. The Society of Indian Psychologists (SIP) filed an amicus brief on behalf of the Native plaintiffs (SIP, 2017). In their brief, SIP included a statement on the intergenerational harm and historical trauma effects of the marginalization of Native populations by governments and their lasting impact (2017). The BIE has filed an appeal (Public Counsel, 2020).

Another lawsuit, adjudicated in 2018, combined two cases, *Louise Martinez, et al., Plaintiffs, v. The State of New Mexico; et al., No. D-101-CV-2014-00793* and *Wilhelmina Yazzie, et al., Plaintiffs, v. The State of New Mexico; et al., No. D-101-CV-2014-02224*. The basis of the case, *Yazzie/Martinez v. State of New Mexico*, was the state failed to provide New Mexico students a sufficient and uniform system as guaranteed by the education clause of the New Mexico State Constitution. The lawsuit contended around 80 percent of the state's 330,000 students were considered at-risk under the law, and included low-income, English-language-learning, and Native American students. The lawsuit also underscored the lack of culturally and linguistically specific education for Indigenous children and English-language learners. An overhaul of the public education system, services, and programs was mandated for the purpose of preparing students to be college, career, and community ready.

These efforts have come a long way from the reference point of the imposition of western education as a process of deliberate submission of Native Peoples. Hopi elders were imprisoned at Alcatraz for resisting the taking of their children by federal agents (R. Pecos, personal communication, September 30, 2020). One of those elders spoke about how white man's education was then, and always would be, our [Native Peoples'] worst enemy (R. Pecos, personal communication, September 30, 2020). In 1895, this elder could not have predicted the peril and full breadth of atrocities and child maltreatment committed against Native children attending institutions of western education.

Alternative Justice Systems

Juvenile delinquency. In some situations, the etiology of juvenile delinquency rests in the school systems. Police resource officers are deployed in many schools, including tribally run schools. The outcomes are two-fold in that these officers' presence protects the school, students, and campus, however the alternative results in using law enforcement action against student conflicts in a very confrontational way. Brayboy expressed his concern stating, "We've brought police into schools with weapons, with a particular kind of training that isn't rooted in who we are as people. . . . It's rooted in conflict resolution in very particular ways; conflict resolution that requires physical force" (personal communication, March 10, 2021). He elaborated that physical force included pepper spray, batons, weapons, and handcuffs or other forms of restraint, which are not meant to be found in educational systems or institutions, and law enforcement is tasked with addressing the issue (personal communication, March 10, 2021). These school incidents are documented in police reports and, consequentially, school interventions become the commencement of these students interfacing with law enforcement entities.

Regardless of the origin of child maltreatment (systemic, institutional, governmental, educational, judicial, or otherwise), research pervasively yields negative outcomes for Native youth (e.g., parental study in chapter 2; incarceration rates for Native adolescents in this chapter; ACEs scores in this chapter; removal of Native children in spite of ICWA; etc.). Aside from the psychological, emotional, and health disparity tolls, some of the behavioral products of child maltreatment are correlated with, but not limited to, physical destructive displays of behavior, aggression, school truancy, juvenile delinquency, substance use, and suicidal ideation (Kastelic, 2013). Consequentially, often these behaviors are a gateway to the judicial system and penal institutions for many Native youth. This point is illustrated in the earlier referenced Havasupai lawsuit wherein:

> The BIE subjected Havasupai schoolchildren like Plaintiff Stephen C. to repeated educational harms at Havasupai Elementary School over a period of years. Instead of getting the educational support and

resources he needed after being diagnosed with ADHD, Stephen C. was pushed out of school and referred to law enforcement. He was routinely sent home early, missing about 50% of instructional time because the school was unable to meet his behavioral and mental health needs, at times only receiving an hour of instructional time a week. (Public Counsel, 2020, para. 7)

Sadly, this case illuminates one example of a Native child's educational needs remaining unmet and law enforcement was saddled with resolving the situation. Situations similar to this occur across Indian Country, thus establishing the foundation for a school to prison pipeline. In addition, when some of these students are referred for mental health interventions, these healthcare systems can become complicit in labeling a child through pathological diagnoses found in the *Diagnostic and Statistical Manual of Mental Disorders*, Fifth Edition (DSM-5), specifically the Disruptive, Impulse-Control, and Conduct Disorder categories.

Contact with police and subsequent arrests are disparate for Native youth in comparison to white youth: 2,251 arrests per 100,000 as compared to 1,793 per 100,000 (Daniel, 2020). In sentencing, presiding judges are often non-Native, and should a jury convene, very few jurors are Native, which has contributed to harsher sentencing for Native Peoples. Ethnic disparities are also prevalent in juvenile justice systems (Rovner, 2016). Native male juveniles are committed to incarceration systems at four times greater than their white counterparts. Native girls (123 per 100,000) are more than four times as likely as white girls to be incarcerated (The Sentencing Project, 2020). Rovner (2016) asserted starting with arrests, a positive relationship exists; racial disparities increase with tiers of the juvenile justice system. Based on Centers for Disease Control and Prevention data, Native Americans are the group most likely to be killed by law enforcement and make up 1.9 percent of police killings (Males, 2014).

As an alternative to punitive systems, restorative justice efforts in tribal communities can assist in precluding the school to prison pipeline that has become prevalent in our society. Western systems of justice mandate some sort of penalty as a consequence, which in a school setting, may reflect detention, suspension, or expulsion for an alleged accusation of wrongdoing (refer to Johnston-Goodstar & VeLure Roholt, 2017). For committing an offense against a community member, the community at large, or violating a law, the punishment may include monetary restitution, incarceration, or death (when sentenced as an adult).

Restorative Justice. Traditional justice systems are discordant with western prosecutorial systems (Lincourt et al., 2021). Western systems are aligned with retributive justice and are punitive. The principles of restorative justice conflict with judicial systems based in a western Eurocentric lens. In a system of restorative justice, the goal is to restore an individual back into the community after a community rule or law was violated. Restorative justice may also be conceptualized as a criminal act or an offense being committed against not only an individual, but the offense also extending to the community (Zion, 1998). In addition, restorative justice may include community leadership, components of kinship, family members of both parties, and aspects of solidarity to resolve conflict and restoring balance (Zion, 1998). In the western system, rules of evidence and procedure do not allow for these parameters. "In the Native worldview there is a deep connection between justice and spirituality: in both, it is essential to maintain or restore harmony and balance" (Mirsky, 2004, p. 1). In the restoration of balance, this traditional system (Lincourt et al., 2021) also includes the intervention of community leadership, thus a hierarchy in the resolution of the offense is not present. The restoration phase may also include a collaborative effort between the family members to determine the penance for the purpose of restoring relationships.

The tenets of restorative justice can be effectively utilized as a systemic way to address offenses juveniles have committed, in alignment with a traditional justice system. In this way, these children are reintegrated back into the community with accountability for their behavior to the community and to the families involved. In addition, placement in a detention facility is averted and interactions with community members are increased, providing a quasi-insulation to not only penal institution exposure, but enhancement of positive skill set building and connectedness in a culturally relevant way. Implementing restorative justice also improves accountability to the community to which they are accountable and in which they reside.

In affiliation with restorative justice, some tribal nations utilize a justice system based in peacemaking (e.g., Navajo Nation). This traditional system of justice may be perceived as harsher for some. Thus, in some situations, because the offender may not choose to confront family and community members, some offenders opt to pursue adjudication of the offense in a western criminal system. However, some tribal communities use a system that engages in a combination of the two systems where a case may be initiated in a formal tribal court, the presiding judge may permit the parties to utilize a restorative justice platform, submit the plan to the court, and monitor the case from afar (June Lorenzo, personal communication, January 27, 2021). At the conclusion of the case, the judge may dismiss the case. Readers may further research restorative justice and/or transformative justice resources cited within the text in this section.

Some school systems have been receptive to restorative justice alternatives. In lieu of contacting law enforcement to address a situation with a student, the school administration will contact the tribe, the tribe intervenes, and the tribe/tribal community resolves the incident. This form of traditional justice also provides reinforcement for components of Native identity (extended family relations), maintains those intimate family connections, sustains a sense of belonging, and assists in establishing the youth's foundational role in the community.

Changing Outcomes

In spite of all the obstacles, Native Peoples are still persevering and working toward justice. As presented in this chapter, there is still much work to do to prevent child maltreatment in systemic, institutional, medical, incarceration, and judicial venues. The protection and safety of Native children requires stricter laws, enforcement of existing laws, holding individuals liable for their actions, and professional accountability for those responsible for the safety of Native children. Deer (2017) stated,

> The federal government must do more to protect tribal members from sexual predators, to safeguard reservations not only from career criminals but also to ensure that federal agencies like the Bureau of Indian Affairs and the Indian Health Services do not hire men with a history of violence against women or children. Further, when attacks

do occur, the federal government must investigate and prosecute these crimes in a timely manner. (p. 799)

Concentrated efforts of multidisciplinary and multijurisdictional teams have been effective in investigatory and prosecutory arenas. Government entities, absent "federal oversight . . . laden with colonial intentions and history" (Deer, 2017, p. 797), must continue to work diligently for the safety and protection of Native children. In terms of therapeutic and community alternatives for Native children, identifying best practices through prevention, intervention, and treatment approaches will be addressed in chapters 5 and 6.

5

Child Maltreatment Best Practices

Implications for Native Children

> One need not have been born
> Native, grown up around Natives,
> or married into a tribe to achieve
> sufficient understanding and
> compassion for their current health
> and well-being. Increasing one's
> cross-cultural competence toward
> another human group is a willful
> and honorable effort.
> —Justin "Doug" McDonald, Oglala
>   Lakota, PhD (2019); UND faculty;
>   director, Indians into Psychology
>   Doctoral Education Program

Child Maltreatment Prevention Programs

There are several Native-focused child maltreatment prevention programs (Linking Actions for Unmet Needs in Children's Health program [LAUNCH]; SafeCare; and Home Visiting programs) that were established as a result of the 2010 Affordable Care Act (ACA) and intervention programs (adapted evidence-based treatments) in collaboration with the National Child Trauma Center. In fact, the Tribal Maternal, Infant, and Early Childhood Home Visiting grant program was established for federally recognized tribes, tribal organizations, and urban Indian organizations (Child Welfare Information Gateway, n.d.). These child maltreatment prevention efforts are situated within the home visiting programs requiring evidence-based strategies that are also culturally relevant and demonstrate evidence of effectiveness (Child Welfare Information Gateway, n.d.). An exploration of these Native-focused child maltreatment prevention and intervention programs will shed light on the critical work being done with Native families. It should be noted the list of programs is not exhaustive, it is limited to those endorsed by the Native elders who were consulted for this book project.

Native Focused Prevention Programs

Project LAUNCH. The purpose of the Project LAUNCH initiative is to promote the well-being of young children (birth to eight years old), through specific grant funding to address the social, emotional, cognitive, physical, and behavioral aspects of their development (National Center for Healthy Safe Children, n.d.). This initiative provides local communities or tribes with the ability to disseminate effective and innovative early childhood mental health practices and services, which lead to better outcomes for young Native children and their families. The overall goal of Project LAUNCH is to foster the healthy development of all young children, preparing them to thrive within the academic setting and beyond. The program is designed to foster the skills of adult caregivers of youth to promote healthy emotional and social development (National Center for Healthy Safe Children, n.d.). Funding for the initiative was established by grants from the Substance Abuse and Mental Health Services Administration (SAMHSA).

Grantees implemented five core prevention and promotion strategies including: 1) screening and assessment in a variety of child-serving settings (e.g., hospitals, care centers), 2) enhanced home visiting through increased focus on social and emotional well-being, 3) mental health consultation in early care and education programs, 4) family strengthening and parent skills training, and 5) integration of behavioral health into primary care settings (National Center for Healthy

Safe Children, n.d.). Funding for the programs allowed grantees to use public health approaches to create more coordinated and collaborative early childhood systems. These programs guided direct services that increased the quality and availability of evidence-based prevention and wellness promotion practices within diverse communities. Grant funding for these unique programs occurred between 2008 until 2016 (National Center for Healthy Safe Children, n.d.).

SafeCare. SafeCare is an evidence-based training curriculum for parents who are at risk or have been reported for child maltreatment (Child Welfare Information Gateway, n.d.). The tenets of the program include receiving weekly home visits to improve skills in the following areas: home safety, health care, and parent-child interactions. Chaffin et al. (2012) conducted two randomized trials that demonstrated the significant benefit of SafeCare to parents compared with services-as-usual (SAU). These individuals received a six-month intensive family preservation program with a case management focus. More than 2,100 enrolled families were followed up for, on average, six years after services. The findings indicated that SafeCare reduced child maltreatment reports by 26 percent (hazard ratio = 0.74), and the authors concluded that SafeCare prevented between 64 and 104 reports per 1,000 cases (assuming a recidivism rate of 45 percent). A subsample of American Indian families from this statewide trial was also found to have lower child welfare recidivism rates among SafeCare families compared with SAU (Chaffin et al., 2012). Additionally, SafeCare was associated with improvement in parental depression and child abuse potential (such that there was decreased potential). Finally, parents receiving SafeCare rated their services higher in cultural competency, working alliance, and satisfaction, indicating this intervention is well received by ethnic minority groups, including Native families (Chaffin et al., 2012).

Another study examined the long-term implications of the cell phone-enhanced parenting intervention of SafeCare (Burke Lefever et al., 2017). The cell phone-supported version of a home visiting program improved long-term parenting practices, maternal depression, and child aggression. The results of the study showed improved parenting skills and lessened child aggression for participating families. Over sixty studies were conducted to develop and validate SafeCare or extensions of the model. In terms of child maltreatment, Lutzker and colleagues compared families receiving SafeCare services to families receiving standard family preservation services in California and found that SafeCare families were significantly less likely to have a recurrence of child maltreatment [15 percent over three years] compared to services-as-usual families [44 percent over three years] (Gershater-Molko et al., 2002; Wesch & Lutzker, 1991). Similar reductions in neglect were found in an evaluation of Project 12-Ways, the predecessor of SafeCare (Wesch & Lutzker, 1991).

Home Visiting Programs. Home visiting programs (e.g., Family Spirit Home Visiting Program, The Nurturing Parenting Programs) offer a variety of family-focused services to expectant parents and families with infants and young children. They include maternal and child health, positive parenting practices, safe home environments, and access to services. Family Spirit Home Visiting Program addresses intergenerational behavioral health issues, instills the application of local cultural assets, and overcomes deficits in the professional health-care workforce in low-resource communities (Center for American Indian Health, n.d.). It is the only evidence-based home-visiting program ever designed for, by, and with AI families. Of note, it is used in over one hundred tribal communities across sixteen states, as well as in various low-income urban neighborhoods in Chicago and St. Louis (Center for American Indian Health, n.d.).

Barlow et al. (2006) assessed the impact of a paraprofessional relived home-visiting intervention to promote childcare knowledge, skills, and involvement among pregnant AI adolescents. The mothers in the intervention group were compared with a control group and were found to have significantly higher parent knowledge at two months and six months postpartum. Additionally, the intervention group mothers scored significantly higher on maternal involvement scales at both two and six months postpartum. Clearly, the intervention was effective for the participants engaged in the program.

The Nurturing Parenting Programs are family-based programs that involve both parents and children in activities that aim to build upon a positive sense of self and respect toward others (Child Welfare Information Gateway, n.d.). There are many programs within this program that are tailored for specific age groups and racial populations. Many of these Home Visiting Programs are identified as cost-effective efforts for promoting infant and child health, preventing maltreatment, and improving family functioning. Home-based programs provide support to build the basic caregiving skills and assist parents as well as other primary caregivers in bonding with children. Another aim of these programs encourages healthy child development and a positive home environment. An exploration of programs for maternal and child health, positive parenting practices, safe home environments, and access to services will further underline the aims of the prevention efforts.

The Birth & Beyond program, one of the Nurturing Parenting Programs (NPP), focuses on ethnically diverse families at considerable risk of child abuse and/or neglect. As the number of NPP lessons was completed, there were corresponding improvements in Child Protective Services (CPS) outcomes (LPC Consulting Associates, 2013). The most vulnerable parents, teens and mothers whose own childhood included abuse and/or neglect, presented the greatest shift in post-program referrals, with very few that resulted in substantiated disposition [3 percent and 7 percent, respectively] (LPC Consulting Associates, 2013). The Birth & Beyond program provides a stable, neighborhood-based resource, in combination with strength-based support, as well as direct service that reinforces good parenting (LPC Consulting Associates, 2013). The program establishes a culturally relevant network of ongoing support for families most at risk for child abuse and/or neglect. The programs that include Native American populations, however, in many cases were not adapted to culturally align with these families. Future studies and programs should include ways that programs might engage in that process. An exploration of interventions that have been adapted for Native American populations is also warranted to understand the contextualized experiences of families impacted by child maltreatment. The following section has excellent examples of evidence-based treatments that have been adapted for Native American populations.

Native Focused Interventions

Native Adaptive Treatments Addressing Child Maltreatment

Trauma has disproportionately impacted Native Americans, creating a specific need for clinical interventions that address the mental health concerns of Native children (BigFoot, 2011). The Indian Country Child Trauma Center (ICCTC) culturally adapted existing evidence-based treatments (EBTs) to integrate AI/AN traditional healing practices, activities, and ceremonies that are used therapeutically to provide instruction about relationships and parenting (ICCTC, 2006). Three Honoring Children interventions (Native Focused Parent-Child Interaction Therapy; Honoring Respectful Ways; and Trauma-Focused Cognitive Behavioral Therapy) developed by the ICCTC were aligned with common and tribal-specific cultural elements to facilitate culturally informed therapies. The University of Oklahoma Health Sciences Center (where ICCTC is located) collaborated with the National Children's Trauma Center and SAMHSA to develop, revise, share, and evaluate culturally informed approaches that were respectful to the tribal variability among Native people while also addressing trauma experiences (BigFoot, 2011). Intervention and prevention models were developed for children and families in Indian Country. A review of the adapted evidence-based treatments for Native Americans will be explored in the following section.

Honoring Children, Making Relatives. Parent-Child Interaction Therapy (PCIT) is the clinical application of techniques aimed at teaching parents how to improve their parenting skills. Honoring Children, Making Relatives (Funderburk et al., 2005) is the clinical application of these parenting techniques within a traditional Native American framework where honor, respect, extended family, instruction, modeling, and teaching were at the center of the process. Furthermore, Honoring Children, Making Relatives integrated parental teachings, practices, rituals, traditions, and cultural beliefs into PCIT, all the while maintaining the guiding principles and theory of PCIT (BigFoot, 2011). An example of these adapted strategies occurs when children exhibit disruptive behaviors or they might be difficult to control and parents may be quick to discipline them. The traditional Native American concept of respect and honor indicates that the adult would be patient, instructive, nonjudgmental, and would use the opportunity to teach (BigFoot, 2011). During PCIT, the parent engages the child through positive interactions, attends to the child, lets the child know they what they are doing right, and eventually instructs the child in good behavior. Honoring Children, Making Relatives facilitates the clinical application of parenting techniques within a traditional Indigenous framework emanating honor, respect, extended family, instruction, modeling, and teaching (BigFoot, 2011).

Honoring Children, Respectful Ways. Silovsky et al. (2005) developed an intervention/prevention curriculum that focuses on honoring and promoting Native children's self-respect, as well as enhances the respect for others, for their elders, for all living creatures, and their environments. It should be noted that a combination of many factors can lead children and youth toward inappropriate sexual behavior [e.g., poor physical boundaries, seeking physical comfort from other children and youth, or touching others' private parts] (BigFoot, 2011). The Honoring Children, Respectful Ways intervention focuses on inappropriate behavior in Native American children and youth and identifies culturally congruent methods of teaching them appropriate ways to honor who they are and promote their Native heritage by utilizing traditional cultural practices (BigFoot, 2011; Silovsky et al., 2005). Some of the core components of the Honoring Children, Respectful Ways protocol include regulations (e.g., respect) about sexual behavior and physical boundaries, age-appropriate sex curriculum, strategies to support the children following and using these rules, and learning skills to manage their behavior. Furthermore, the skills include feeling identification, relaxation, coping, problem solving, impulse control, abuse prevention, and social relationship skills (BigFoot, 2011; Silovsky et al., 2005). The program can be experienced as either an intervention or prevention designed to connect Native American children and their families to their traditional ways and practices, with the aims of developing positive beliefs about themselves, healthy values and behaviors in their relationships with others (BigFoot, 2011).

Honoring Children, Mending the Circle. A final model is trauma-focused cognitive behavioral therapy (TF-CBT), which combines trauma-informed interventions with elements of cognitive behavioral therapy to create a treatment aimed to address the unique needs of children with PTSD and other problems related to traumatic life events (BigFoot, 2011). Honoring Children, Mending the Circle (BigFoot & Schmidt, 2012) provides the clinical application of TF-CBT with a traditional Indigenous framework aligned with Native cultural models of well-being. The core concept is the TF-CBT "cognitive triangle," which clarifies the connection between one's emotions, thoughts, and behaviors (BigFoot, 2011). In Native American culture, well-being is considered a healthy balance between and within the spiritual, relational, physical, emotional, and mental aspects of life, both individually and collectively (BigFoot, 2011).

While trauma creates imbalance, healing moves to restore balance and harmony, both within and between aspects of the person's life (BigFoot, 2011). The "trauma narrative" is another critical component of TF-CBT, which entails a structured and repetitive re-sharing of the traumatic event in order to gradually expose the child to the traumatic memory (BigFoot, 2011; BigFoot & Schmidt, 2012). The gradual exposure process works to lessen the child's emotional reactivity to the trauma memory. In the Honoring Children, Mending the Circle model it incorporates gradual exposure into the healing process through a selection of culturally informed therapeutic approaches (BigFoot & Schmidt, 2012). Traditional Native American ceremonies and healing practices include components of gradual exposures through oral tradition and storytelling as forms of cognitive restructuring. Additionally, Sweat Lodge, with the increase of heated rocks with each round of songs and prayers, can be experienced as healing (BigFoot, 2011; BigFoot & Schmidt, 2012). The Honoring Children, Mending the Circle well-being model is based on tribal teachings of a circle with intersecting parts, and it remains flexible to accommodate individuals from diverse cultures, spiritual backgrounds, and religious beliefs (BigFoot & Schmidt, 2008; BigFoot, 2011). The model can be tailored to incorporate the factors that are culturally relevant for participating families (e.g., tribally specific values, beliefs, practices, or customs). Considerations for new ways to experience treatment and ways of living have been proposed. Exploring a shift in how the field of psychology conceptualizes treatment includes elements of liberation through radical healing.

Challenges to Treatment

Challenges to treatment when working with a Native child and Native family are extensive. In many treatment settings for Native constituents across the U.S., there is a dearth of culturally competent providers and culturally relevant theoretical models; cultural humility approaches to treatment are even rarer. Cookie cutter treatment, manualized treatment, and evidence-based therapies normed on dominant society populations are generally ineffective without adaptation, or do not work, as they are missing essential cultural components. Most western treatment models are based on individualistic treatment paradigms and catapult the construct of autonomy to the forefront. Autonomy, in the majority of western based practice approaches, is the goal of successful treatment. However, it is antitheoretical and generally contraindicated to the collectivistic nature of Native children and families.

Domains of Holistic Consideration

Worldview

Manualized evidence-based treatments do not take into consideration collectivistic cultural nuances and exclude Native traditional values. From an Indigenous lens, health and wellness are conceptualized from a holistic perspective and disharmony or imbalance connote pathology (McDonald et al., 2019). Often, the dominant society frames Native health and wellness assets negatively and contradictorily conceptualizes health, including unhealthy behaviors, as positive (Hodge & Limb, 2010). Treatment efficacy rapidly depreciates when treatment modalities are not culturally relevant and the worldview of the provider does not make allowances for the Native patient.

Acculturation

If a provider does not assess the child's and/or family's level of acculturation, this can lead to devastating outcomes for the Native child, thereby creating monumental challenges to treatment. Though extraordinary, Native communities still exist in the United States wherein the Native language of origin is the child's first language. The provider's efforts, attempting to provide treatment interventions based in a western model, will undoubtedly end in disastrous outcomes due to the incompatibility of worldviews and perspectives. In fact, without assessing the acculturation of the child and family, the provider may further traumatize the Native child and family by utilizing such an approach (McDonald et al., 1993). In addition, the end result may be the wounding of the soul of the child (Duran, 2006; Duran et al., 2008), which may further exacerbate treatment ineffectiveness. The acculturation component of treatment alludes to the identity of the Native child, whose identity may be in flux, in consideration of the systemic and institutional confounds as presented in chapter 2 and risk factors in chapter 3.

Trust

Mental health treatment can also be impeded by a well-founded distrust in the mental health (Willeto, 2014), medical, and overall governmental systems. The removal of Native children from their communities has spanned history for a multitude of reasons (review chapter 2 for further explanation), and underlies the basis for this wariness. In contemporary times, many children and family members have witnessed a Native child's removal from the home for unsubstantiated allegations of neglect. Thus, there is an immediate resistance and hesitancy to cooperate with mental health, medical, and government entities. "Although hard data are not available, clinical experience suggests that the majority of Indian families have lost one or more children to the non-Indian child welfare system" (Swinomish Tribal Mental Health Project, 1991, p. 29).

Access to Care

As noted previously, the geography of Indian Country includes remote and rural topography. Thus, access to treatment providers and treatment settings is a significant barrier to treatment. Geographic hardships are very tangible when a child needs mental health or medical treatment and the family must navigate travel several hours away to the nearest care center. As cited before, socioeconomic limitations can impede fuel purchases or ownership of a vehicle for travel to a clinic and/or as in Alaska, where road systems do not exist, the purchase of a plane ticket to travel for care is often unaffordable. In many remote and rural health facilities, access to providers specializing in child treatment and interventions is non-existent. Further, though telehealth has become more necessary in the COVID pandemic, many Native communities across the nation lack basic internet capability as the infrastructure does not yet exist.

Psychometric Testing

In relation to evidence-based practice (EBP) and evidence-based treatment (EBT) models, psychometric testing instrumentation is generally not normed with the inclusion of Native Peoples. Thus, the results of these standardized tests are skewed, create a "so-called achievement gap" (Brayboy & Chin, 2020, p. 25), and stigmatize Native children for the duration of their youth, as observed by the first author who has served in remote and rural tribal communities. She rewrote psychological evaluations to reconceptualize interpretations of western psychological tests that often pathologize Native children. Circumstances in a child's life were also interpreted from a Native psychologist's lens wherein protective factors (refer to chapter 3) were highlighted from a strength-based perspective. In the utilization of standardized testing instruments, it is imperative the results are interpreted within a cultural context; not doing so contributes to the concept of scientific racism (McDonald & Chaney, 2003) and disenfranchises Native children. This includes personality testing, which can convert cultural norms into pathological results. Another important consideration in the interpretation of psychometric test results should include the quality of education the Native child has attained. Chapters 2 and 3 extensively reported the underprivileged educational experiences of Native children historically and contemporarily, which likely exacerbate poor standardized tests and scoring. McDonald et al. recommend the following:

(a) honestly evaluate your own level of cultural competence and, if necessary, increase and adapt it appropriately; (b) exercise significant caution when choosing and using standardized tests insufficiently normed for those on which you intend to use them; (c) consider differential levels of cultural orientation and competence (and thereby the appropriateness) of the patients or participants you intend to assess with these instruments; and (d) indicate clearly in any dissemination of assessment findings the limitations of using such instruments on these particular patients or participants (APA, 2002; Dana, 1993; McDonald & Chaney, 2003). Although these suggestions are necessary, they are by no means sufficient to ensure the responsible and psychometrically sound use of standardized tests with American Indian patients or participants.

Data

In terms of data, Suina (2017) discussed the methods in which data is reported, citing a U.S. government health statistics study wherein the data collected further perpetuated stereotypes of Native peoples [e.g., "the drunken Indian,"] (p. 91). Research in Indian Country, obtaining representative, accurate data of the population under investigation, is better amassed through research methods inclusive of the community and conducted with tribal participation. Methods such as community based participatory research and qualitative research methods have been beneficial and had promising success for both the researchers and community. Tribes have also decreed their sovereign authority as it pertains to acquired data, including traditional knowledge.

These considerations lend themselves to an enormous challenge to treatment for Native children and families, as stigmatizing statistical data disadvantages Native peoples. These are the types of reports and materials mainstream scholars, providers, educators, and/or systemic/institutional representatives search, learn, absorb, and depend on, consequently clouding their judgement and delivery of services to Native children and families. In some cases, this data sets the foundation for Indian Country mainstream providers' attitudes and approaches to "fix" the Native client/patient and has resulted in systemic and experimental child maltreatment.

Tribes have begun to legislate research procedures, process, and data release to counteract this influence. Rodriguez-Lonebear (2016) stated, "Tribal data are perhaps the most valuable tools of self-determination because they drive tribal nation-building by tribes for tribes" (as cited in Chaney, 2018), thus there are enormous implications in tribal entities legislating all forms of data collection and access to outside entities. In 2010, the Tribal Law and Order Act was enacted, which created a bidirectional sharing of data between the government and tribes (Chaney, 2018). Of note, background checks for authorized tribes are conducted in hiring of individuals having control or access to children through the Next Generation Identification system, which is managed by the FBI Criminal Justice Information Services Division (Chaney, 2018).

Summary

Recently, there has been a focus on early childhood interventions in Indian Country. In some states, such as in New Mexico, there has been a concentrated effort to provide comprehensive support to families with prevention and intervention strategies for promotion of health and well-being for babies and toddlers. These efforts are wholly focused on healthier children and families, thereby reducing the potential for negative social, interpersonal, and parental effects. As noted in this chapter, there are multiple challenges to treatment, influenced by historical events, but these challenges also include contemporary circumstances, many resting in intergenerational, well-founded distrust in systems and institutions. Much work has yet to be done. An introduction to culturally relevant approaches is introduced in chapter 6. The existence of contemporary ethical considerations should guide future work when addressing child maltreatment.

6

Contemporary Cultural and Ethical Issues in Child Maltreatment

> Offering water up before the first drink of the day in gratitude for the gift of water, acknowledging all those who go without water to strengthen their spirit, remembering those who don't have good water and want it, praying for those who have too much water.
> —Dolores Subia BigFoot, Caddo Nation, PhD, and Iva GreyWolf, Ft. Peck Assiniboine, PhD (2014)

This chapter starts with relevant advocacy and intervention strategies, and positive strategies to counter effects of child maltreatment. These strategies include an Indigenist coping model, dialogue on child welfare reform, a curriculum for life skills with cultural component inclusion, and a positive prevention program for AI youth. The contextual factors influencing Native American children's experiences of child maltreatment will be explored. Although there are some historical issues that carry over to the present, child maltreatment in the AI/AN population remains complex and deserves a deconstructed approach. We will examine selected cultural and ethical issues in consideration of cumulative trauma (chapter 2), present-day risk factors (chapter 3), and exigent factors (chapter 4).

In individuals identifying singularly as American Indian or Alaska Native (AI/AN), youth under the age of twenty-five comprise approximately 42 percent of the overall population, numbering about 1.2 million; over 33 percent are under the age of eighteen (National Congress of American Indians [NCAI], 2021a). In 2016, there were an estimated 676,000 victims of abuse and neglect, approximating a national rate of 9.1 victims per 1,000 children in the U.S. population (U.S. Department of Health & Human Services, 2018). The estimated associated costs for child maltreatment in the United States are $428 billion a year (Peterson et al., 2018). Most reported victims were of three races/ethnicities: Whites (44.9 percent), Latinx/Hispanic (22.0 percent), and African American (20.7 percent), though AI/AN children had the highest rate of victimization at 14.2 per 1,000 children in the population of the same race or ethnicity (U.S. Department of Health & Human Services, 2018).

This indicator segues into current statistics reported on a national average, as AI/ANs are more likely to experience violent crimes at a rate of 2.5 times higher and are two times more likely to be the crime victims of rape or sexual assault compared to all other racial/ethnic groups (NCAI, 2021b). Some statistics overlap pertaining to teen years, however over the lifespan, it is estimated 56.1 percent of AI/AN women will experience sexual violence and 84.3 percent of AI/AN women will experience violence in their lifetime (NCAI, 2021b). Regarding AI/AN youth, according to Cross (2020), they will "experience longer stays in out-of-home care, greater numbers of placements, and a greater likelihood of aging out of care rather than returning to their families, being adopted, or finding legal guardianship" (p. 102). These circumstances speak to the necessity of sensitivity when working with Native children and families, understanding the complexity of the Native child and family, and advocating on behalf of Native children.

Countering Child Maltreatment

From a Native lens, when addressing child maltreatment in western systems and circles, the issue becomes a zero-sum game for the non-Native system agency, with a winner and loser, and a potential activation of power, control, and criticism. Consequently, what tends to happen is the focus on what is in the best interest of the Native child becomes lost. In these situations, assumptions are made about the Native child/family and life-changing decisions are made hastily, without thoroughly evaluating the unique circumstances. Ethically, professionals and social welfare employees interacting with the children have a duty to contemplate the outcomes of their decisions and attenuate to the law, such as with the removal of legal guardianship or placement of a Native child, in consideration of the Indian Child Welfare Act, for example. Healing trauma and maltreatment created by systems and institutions may be lifelong journeys for the affected individuals, especially when this trauma commences in childhood. We are advocating for collaborative approaches to healing for Native children, using both traditional healing and western therapeutic services, as the health and well-being of Native children is not a zero-sum game.

Positive Strategies

"Indigenist" Stress Coping Paradigm. A majority of research aligned with stress coping centers on Eurocentric values, conceptual structures, and methodologies that do not pertain to Native populations. Upon applying them, researchers increase the risk of oppressing the Native communities they intend to serve and limit the outcome of the findings (Walters et al., 2002). A more appropriate plan of action in Native communities includes considering their sociohistorical experiences and an evaluating of their impact. An Indigenous perspective identifies the colonized position of Indigenous peoples residing within the United States and advocates for their sovereignty as well as empowerment in a postcolonial world (Walters et al., 2002). Walters, et al., (2002) provide a framework for understanding how Native Americans cope with traumatic life stressors exacerbated by colonization.

Furthermore, they advocate that research with Natives be contextualized by assessing the impact of the distress (e.g., colonization) on mental health and health-related issues (e.g., substance use, diabetes). The model posits that associations between traumatic life stressors and adverse health outcomes are moderated by cultural factors (e.g., cultural practices, traditional medicine), protective factors that might serve as buffers, potentially strengthening emotional and psychological health while mitigating the effects of the traumatic distress (Walters et al., 2002). Additionally, acknowledging the barriers to care (e.g., limited availability, access to services, and transportation challenges) as well as avoidance of care related to the potential for justifiable fear of discrimination might lead to adverse health consequences. The model fits well in the conceptualization of Native child maltreatment, as it acknowledges cultural practices and ways of knowing that might mitigate some of their lived experiences.

Touchstones of Hope. The National Indian Child Welfare Association and First Nations Child and Family Caring Society of Canada have collaborated on a Touchstones of Hope training series and dialogue to address the welfare of Indigenous children and reform the child welfare system. The Touchstones of Hope movement was born in 2005. The discussions, held with many nations, centered on the exploration of child welfare history, examining the reasons for an increase in Indigenous children entering the child welfare system, and reshaping the child welfare system. The movement was also dependent on a reconciliation process that included:

> Indigenous and non-Indigenous people truth telling about the harm the child welfare system has done to families, acknowledging a new path forward, restoring by making changes to redress harm and ensure it doesn't happen again, and relating by working respectfully together toward our vision of a new system. (NICWA, 2021, para. 5)

This reconciliation process was guided by five principles: self-determination, culture and language, holistic approach, structural interventions, and non-discrimination (NICWA, 2021). In addressing the historical and contemporary circumstances of overall Native child welfare in various platforms at multiple systemic levels, the potential for meaningful change exists. This effort is noteworthy in that it contributes to a reparative process among AI/AN populations as well as foreign governments.

Project Venture. Project Venture was an outdoor experiential youth program for at-risk youth that was first fully implemented in 1990 by the National Indian Youth Leadership Project (NIYLP). The program served over 4,000 AI youth in New Mexico and was adopted in more than fifty AI and other communities throughout the United States. Project Venture, whose initial focus was on substance abuse prevention, continues to flourish and has evolved into several program adaptations. In 2015, NIYLP partnered with a SAMHSA affiliated program, National Network to Eliminate Disparities in Behavioral Health (NNED), which provided funding opportunities for a three-day Project Venture training for communities. So far, there have been nine Canadian provinces that have implemented the program and it has expanded into twenty-five U.S. states with at least seventy community implementations (National Network to Eliminate Disparities in Behavioral Health, 2022).

Radical Healing Model. Exploring new ways Native American children and families might become liberated through therapy is critical during these times. We are currently navigating our way through a pandemic, socio-political unrest, and racial injustices (e.g., murders of Black, Indigenous and People of Color [BIPOC] at elevated rates, sustained anti-Asian sentiment and violence). French et al. (2020) posit that radical healing is grounded within the context of the psychology of liberation, ethnopolitical psychology, Black psychology, and intersectionality. They further report radical healing being situated within a dialectic and that it exists in both spaces of resisting oppression and moving toward freedom (French et al., 2020), suggesting that remaining at the extremes of the dialect is detrimental to individuals (e.g., Native children and families should strive for balance).

The idea of radical healing might be reflected in treatment through collaborating with children and families to measure outcomes as they progress in therapy through an exploration of Indigenous wellness (examining the meaningfulness of engaging in this type of process, what it means culturally for their family to be well, and the impact of their well-being in relation to their community). Additional aspects of radical healing can include exploring various ways of engaging in the therapeutic experience (e.g., acknowledging ancestors in treatment and honoring them during their therapeutic journeys) and integrating advocacy (e.g., participation in protest) as a form of healing (Ramos et al., in press). Essentially, the client should acknowledge who is empowering them as they accomplish certain treatment goals or who might also be healed as they are healed. The practitioners might also engage Native children and families in their community (contributing to collective healing). These and other ideas encompass a decolonized approach to therapy that can challenge the systems of oppression within the field of psychology and directly acknowledges People of Color's (POCs) learned and lived experiences, which demand an intersectional lens to comprehend the healing process (French et al., 2020).

Healing Approaches

Culture as a Healing Mechanism. Practice of cultural ways, alone or in combination with western services, can ameliorate the effects of traumatic experiences (Tehee et al., 2021). Western providers do not have to possess knowledge of traditional healing mechanisms. However, the encouragement of participation in these forms of healing praxis can contribute to the overall healing of the child, rather than a child experiencing feelings of unnecessary dissonance or pressure in having to make a choice, as posed by western systems. The practice of cultural ways has been used since the beginning of time by Indigenous Peoples (Tehee et al., 2021) and continues to sustain the Native populations. Advocacy for traditional practices in healing journeys have been supported by numerous Native professionals and scholars including Dr. Justin "Doug" McDonald, Dr. Iva GreyWolf, Dr. Joseph Gone, Dr. Bryan McKinley James Brayboy, Dr. Dolores Subia BigFoot, Dr. Melissa Tehee (their scholarly works may be found in the reference section).

Narrative Therapy. Narrative therapy is culturally compatible in working with Native Peoples, as this approach is congruent with traditional healing pedagogies and ontologies (Tehee et al., 2021). Traditional talking circles and the oral tradition continue to be utilized in tribal communities (Gone & Kirmayer, 2020; Tehee et al., 2021) and are compatible with a relational and collectivistic orientation. Components of narrative therapy also permit the Native client to relate the details of their trauma in an unstructured, non-rigid format, which can potentially increase the comfort level of the client in a western-based mental health setting.

Cognitive Behavior Therapy. Quantitative studies have been conducted with the use of cognitive behavior therapy (CBT) in Native populations. Research outcomes have yielded both positive and negative results.

However, CBT can be effectively adapted for Native clients and students with the inclusion of cultural components (see Duran et al., 2008; McDonald et al., 2018, 2019) and cognitive behavioral interventions for trauma in schools (Morsette et al., 2009).

Contemporary Ethical Issues

Native American Identity

One of the greatest threats to Native children today relates to the identity of Native children. Chapters 2 and 3 allude to the importance of their overall health and well-being in consideration of the role of culture. AI/AN identity is inherently linked to land, and feminine identity emerges or is birthed by the land. While gender roles shift over time, European contact resulted in an imposition of gendered ideals that conflicted with Native American ideals about gender (Slater & Yarbrough, 2012). Prior to European contact, Native American women were identified as extensions of tribal spiritual guides, as the stronger healers within communities, and the keepers of the legacy of their families. Native societies of the past were not founded on hierarchical or patriarchal systems and the gender divisions that existed were either fluid or were considered sacred.

While Native women and men held different responsibilities and roles in their contributions to the community, Native women were held in deep respect and valued for their special ways of knowing, particularly around the survival and success of the community (Bigfoot & GreyWolf, 2014; Popick, 2006). Strong and persistent Native families and their communities can collectively protect Native children against the harms of systematic racism. The degree to which families and their communities have instilled positive messages about their cultural identity and heritage, despite a history of poor treatment, is a predictor of healthy development in adolescents of color (Neblett et al., 2012). Future research must continue to include diversity, particularly around the intersection of gender and ethnicity.

Cumulative Trauma

Another consideration related to contemporary child maltreatment is associated with trauma: complex, primary, secondary, tertiary, and vicarious. In the health, psychological, and medical sciences, there is a convenient tendency to deduce and compartmentalize trauma into spliced pockets without acknowledgment of intergenerational comorbidities. At times, this has been used to stratify the traumas Native children endured for the purpose of institutions and systems to say, "It wasn't that bad," or "It could have been worse." "Trauma . . . is trauma" (Bigfoot, 2020, p. 11) and beginning the narrative of as part of the holistic imbalance from a Native perspective can truly begin the healing process. Dr. Delores Subia Bigfoot (2020) contended, "Tribal communities have been trauma informed forever, and it's a term that we are just now using as it is being exposed as trauma exposure and secondary exposure" (p. 12).

To put this concept into perspective, the following example minimally captures the plight of the Native child in a very simplistic scenario: the child attends kindergarten in a public school and is instructed they must communicate in English only (in opposition, there are consequences); the child learns in third grade Columbus "discovered" their ancestors; in fifth grade, they are taught North America was inhabited by their ancestors who crossed a now nonexistent land bridge; in middle school, they learn about Darwin's natural selection and remnants of Garth's (1927) intelligence strata in correlation to their degree of Indian blood; and in high school, more about "Kill the Indian, save the man." In reflection, how is this not trauma and child maltreatment as it pertains to the Native child? But yet, this is the modern curriculum in state-operated public schools, *even* in tribal communities with one hundred percent Native students. DiAngelo (2018) asserted, "Racism is a structure not an event" (p. 27), which perpetuates ongoing standardized educational racism in today's classrooms. This narrative in systemic and institutional forums must radically change to include an acknowledgement of the history of Native peoples and other ethnic minority groups. Courageous conversations with policy makers must impact an overhaul of the education system for healthy psychosocial development of children and equity of all children served, as these aforementioned scenarios in a Native child's life contribute to ongoing historical trauma.

Historical Trauma and Contemporary Impact

Historical trauma is aligned with the cumulative and collective effects, both across an individual life course and across generations, of deaths due to conflict and disease, forced removal of communities from their tribal communities, systemic sexual and physical abuse of

Native American children in communities and boarding schools, forced or coerced cultural assimilation, and contamination of Native American lands including sacred sites (Brave Heart & Debruyn, 1998; Burrage, 2018; Campbell & Evans-Campbell, 2011; Evans-Campbell, 2008; Kirmayer et al., 2014). Historical Trauma has implications for contributing to many contemporary health and mental health challenges including but not limited to elevated rates of anxiety and depressive disorders, post-traumatic stress disorder (PTSD), substance use disorders, intimate partner violence, child maltreatment, and diabetes (Campbell & Evans-Campbell, 2011; Evans-Campbell, 2008). Evans-Campbell (2008) suggested that the effect of traumatic events can be analyzed at the community level and may include a breakdown of values and culture, high rates of alcohol abuse, physical ailments, social malaise, and weakened social structures. Campbell and Evans-Campbell (2011) furthered the discussion to include the impacts of child development at the individual and family levels, as well as weakening social networks and a decreased sense of safety as well as solidarity (Kirmayer et al., 2014).

The above-mentioned factors framed the experiences of many Native American children who were stolen from their families and sent to boarding school institutions, as has been iterated. They were treated inhumanely, abused physically, sexually, and psychologically, and some never returned home to their tribal homelands and died alone in places foreign to them (review chapter 2 for an overview). Native peoples, especially children, have been viewed as property, savages, or less than, due to their status as government wards. Government agents and the dominant society over time have perceived Natives as not being human. Therefore, stealing or killing a Native person was of no consequence. Terminology referring to Native peoples such as "savage" or "dirty" affirmed these stereotypes (Tehee & Green, 2017).

The results of intergenerational community trauma continue to be experienced today and in Alaska, precede statehood. Consider the lives of an entire generation of youth who suffered severe sexual abuse in St. Michael, Alaska, a remote village in northwest Alaska. Almost the entire village of St. Michael's children, 156 children who came forward as adults, were molested by two priests and a clergy layman (Curran, 2011). However, another news story also identified nine Jesuit affiliated personnel (Hopkins, 2019) who committed the abuse between 1949 and 1987. None of the sexually abusive clergy were ever criminally charged, in these cases or in other clergy abuses in U.S. tribal communities nationwide; in fact, many were allowed to retire on the Gonzaga University campus (Schwing et al., 2018).

As an adult, Elsie Boudreau, one of the victims abused for almost ten years, filed a lawsuit after non-acknowledgment of her report by the church. Kenneth Roosa, attorney for Ms. Boudreau, stated, "This was 1970. It was absolutely unthinkable that the Catholic church could be involved in the sexual abuse of children. There was nowhere for the kids to hide. There was no one they could talk to. The adults believed the abusers over their own children. It was a perfect storm for molestation." In totality, almost 150 individuals joined the lawsuit. The circumstances of these tragic events were documented in a PBS special entitled "The Silence" (2011).

The people of St. Michael have continued to practice songs and dances passed down from generation to generation. After all this community experienced, reflection on the word "resilient" is an underestimation of the resulting grief, tragedy, and loss of life in a multitude of ways. At present, Elsie Boudreau speaks of her survivorship with positivity (McBride, 2020). Her words are powerful in application of psychological understandings of trauma and demonstrates the essence of self-determination and resistance through testimony. A Native reporter, Mark Trahant, covered the story of the molestation case. He noted the following:

> My favorite experience in St. Michael was a night of traditional songs and dances. What else here radiates as bright as the sun? How about those moments when a community comes together as it has for several thousand years? The songs, stories, and dances that made ancestors smile still do. It's that resilience of spirit, of a people being together, that surfaced as fast as the sunrise. You can see the dawn in people's faces. (2011, para. 11–12)

Although there is a sense of positivity and protectiveness in the response of the AN Peoples in this community, it is more likely for children to be removed from AN parents and guardians in this same community than the charging and prosecution of non-Native sexual abuse offenders. Ethically, one must wonder how this egregious abuse of law, order, and justice can exist at this time in the United States. As a society, we must collaborate for equity and parity.

Native Gendered-Based Stereotypes and Gender-Based Violence

Deconstruction

Historical. Native women and girls have continuously been exploited, romanticized as the Indian Princess (Tehee & Green, 2017), and brutalized since foreign contact by colonizers, during westward expansion, by Indian agents, and through widespread rape committed by military men as a form of warfare (Deer, 2017). Many of the historical stereotypical presentations and racist attitudes persist, affecting the psychological well-being of modern Native Americans, as there remains a persistent legacy of a 500-year history of oppression and prejudice. These factors begin to establish a basis for violence against Native women and girls, through the deconstruction of a woman and reconstruction of her in the form of a sexualized object (Tehee & Green, 2017), and through the hypersexualization of interpersonal relationships and traditional gender roles (Gutierrez, 1991). In addition, Minthorn (2018) stated:

> Settlers' interactions with the community included the physical violation of many women through rape or trade of women for something of "value," resulting in the dehumanization of women in our communities. (p. 63)

Interpersonal Violence. The operational definitions of domestic violence and intimate partner violence are considerations in the discussion. Domestic violence is perceived differently by Native women in comparison to European American (EA) women, as highlighted in a study conducted by Tehee and Esqueda (2008). Native women defined domestic violence as being perpetuated in a physical form, wherein EA women included physical and internally driven motivations identified as emotional and verbal expressions as well. A research study cohort of Native men concluded that "the process of forced assimilation and contact with colonizing groups was the major cause of contemporary social problems of IPV and alcoholism" (Matamonasa-Bennett, 2015, p. 27).

Patriarchy. Pre-contact, intimate partner violence was not a part of relations between Native men and women (Matamonasa-Bennett,

2015, 2017; Tehee & Esqueda, 2008). Generally, traditional gender roles within tribal structures were egalitarian. The roles were associated with specific responsibilities. A social structure also existed in Native communities wherein a prescribed social code was paramount and averted conflict and victimization. Community members respected this social code, which incited order with banishment from the tribe as the ultimate penalty for violation (Smith, 2017).

Contemporarily, as gender roles have evolved and Native societies have changed to meet the demands, gender roles have had to adapt. This transition may be reflected in the workforce where both parents need to work, as both parent's incomes are required to meet family financial needs. However, ceremonially, the traditional structural roles remain the same and have changed minutely, if at all. In the literature, this delineation in roles has been perceived as women being secondary or substandard to men. However, this is an inaccurate interpretation of Native cultural norms.

Sociocultural Influences

Stereotypes

Media. Accurate portrayals of Native Peoples in the media remain scant. Most members of the U.S. public have difficulty naming contemporary Native Americans because representations in typical media outlets and popular culture as members of the current society are lacking (Tehee & Green, 2017). In fact, for many, Native Americans exist only as a memory of a group of people preserved (typically inaccurately) within movies, television, and history textbooks. The broad strokes of these stereotypes are historically gendered and impact not only the way others treat Native Americans but also how Native Americans may view themselves, their identity, and possibilities for their future (e.g., family, education, and careers) (Tehee & Green, 2017). These stereotypes are different for Native Americans compared with other racial and ethnic groups in the United States as they are still rooted in the past and lead to more overt racism.

Additionally, media exposure promoting negative images, stereotypes, and negative news about Native people reinforces stereotypes and essentially normalizes violence. These depictions also contribute to the psychological burden on Native populations who are exposed to messages that insinuate their inferior status. A Native scholar, remaining anonymous, imparted, "There is also an issue of hearing that your relatives are 'savages' in history class or when you see a popular movie with cowboys and Indians—when I was growing up. I went home and asked my mom if my relatives were 'savages.' I really started questioning everything I was learning."

Environmental Injustices—Connection to Land

Environmental Trauma

Injustice. Another one of the most damaging threats to the Native child today pertains to the environmental injustices occurring in real time. The environmental traumas from the Dakota Access Pipeline (DAPL) at Standing Rock, South Dakota (Brayboy & Chin, 2020; Isaacs et al., 2020; McDonald et al., 2019) and the oil boom in western North Dakota are currently unfolding in our nation. In addition, one can discover the most recent environmental threats by perusing national media feeds. There are several considerations related to this issue, including sovereignty, pillaging of the land, and the spiritual and religious connotations for the Native child. As alluded to in the previous chapters, the overall health and mental well-being of the Native child is related to the holism of the mind, body, and spirit (McDonald et al., 2019) with intimate relationships in the cosmological and the ecological spheres. Thus, the onslaught of mining, oil extraction, and other events disfiguring Mother Earth have distressed the ecological balance of space and place for many.

This issue further extends to the restraint of hunting and fishing rites of Native peoples, thereby influencing a way of life through restriction of traditional activities for the Native child. One may ponder how this applies to child maltreatment. Throughout the years, the rites of Native peoples to engage in a subsistence livelihood have been impacted by loss of land masses, control by government regulatory agencies, and encroachment of residential living spaces by dominant society expansion. Through limited avenues to regain some control over their ancestral way of living, Native peoples have had to resort to litigation at local, state, and federal levels. Native ceremonial practices are closely related to the exercise of these rites.

Further, in such places as Alaska, where the cost of living is astronomical, living a subsistence lifestyle is imperative for the survival of many families. However, due to the regulatory mandates now in place, individuals must abide by laws that were not written by Native people, because non-Natives exploited the once plentiful game and fish. Historically, these activities (hunting and fishing) were what parents and relations did with youth, and even now there is a push to get back to those traditional ways and re-engage the youth. Gradually taking away these rites, as well as poisoning the land, impacts our traditions and hence our parenting.

Food Deserts. Many tribal lands are remote (e.g., Alaska Native villages, Navajo Nation) and considered food deserts. Due to the remoteness, nutritional foods and vegetables are difficult to access and often, foods and beverages with high sugar, starch, and sodium are much more affordable and available. Consider the first author's first trip to a grocery store in the far northwest region of Alaska where one-quarter of a watermelon was almost $25.00! Limited food options lead to food insecurity and increase the risk of obesity, diabetes, hypertension, and cancer, all health concerns highly prevalent among Native Americans (Blue Bird Jernigan et al., 2017).

Research that analyzed food insecurity trends of AI/ANs compared to other racial and ethnic groups in the United States from 2000 to 2010 found that 25 percent of Native Americans remained consistently food insecure (Blue Bird Jernigan et al., 2017). Additionally, the AI/AN population was twice as likely to be food insecure compared to whites, while urban Native Americans were more likely to experience food insecurity than rural Natives. This research advocates for national and tribal policies that expand food assistance programs; promotes and supports increased access to healthy foods; and calls for community food security in both rural and urban areas. Ethically, more work needs to be done to reduce the burden of diet-related health disparities on low income and racial/ethnic minority populations, such that these individuals can regularly access healthy food options for their families.

Summary

Culturally relevant approaches and practice-based evidence have been most effective in Native communities, although there is a dearth of empirical studies in this area. These methodologies are inclusive of

Native ontologies and pedagogies, which, in reflection, translate to the resurrection of traditional medicinal knowledge and wisdoms enacted in Native communities. This is not to propose traditional knowledge is superior to western knowledge, but to affirm the orthogonal and egalitarian relationships in healing. Systems and institutions, education and therapeutic approaches, and law and policy, should acknowledge the integration of traditional Indigenous knowledge and methodologies for healing and edification. Advocacy and calls to action will be further addressed in chapter 7.

7
Bringing It All Together

Not about Us without Us

> It is wholly ironic that the deliberate
> intent of colonizers to eliminate
> Indigenous cultures not only did
> not succeed but proves to be the
> foundational heart upon which
> their well-being flourishes.
> —Dr. Angela A. A. Willeto (2014)

Navigating through this book may have triggered trauma and feelings of uncomfortableness. As Native People, throughout the historical and contemporary exemplifications, we have endured countless injustices. It has been incumbent upon us to find ways to heal ourselves, beyond the bounds of resilience. For many, our healing journeys remain embedded in everyday lived experiences and the practice of our traditional ways. Many of those who have lost their traditional practices through cultural genocide have had to adapt and borrow from other Indigenous groups. Others have implemented practices of re-traditionalization. And yet others are in an indeterminate state, rediscovering and unmasking obscured traditional practices without fear of retribution by church, state, or governmental officials.

In illuminating life experiences of Native Peoples, we have brought forward a call for action. These issues must be taken into the arenas of policy and law for equity and parity for the original inhabitants of the United States. During all the years Willis, DeLeon, Haldane, and Heldring (2014) have helped to shape public policy, they emphasized personal involvement as being the key factor in effecting substantial change. As professionals and scholars, we may have some help in the upcoming years. At present, there is a "large bubble" in the fifteen to nineteen-year-old American Indian and Alaska Native (AI/AN) age group, thus their voices will likely soon influence voting, college admissions, graduations (NCAI, 2021a), and effect meaningful changes in law and policy relevant to Native children, families, and communities.

The hope of reformation and change is exemplified by the history being made in 2021 with President Joe Biden's appointment, and the congressional confirmation of Debra Haaland, Pueblo of Laguna, as the first Native person serving as the 54th United States Secretary of the Interior. Reformation and change can also be seen in the many psychologists, scholars, professionals, paraprofessionals, and grassroots community groups, all working toward the common goal of supporting Native children, families, and communities. All the love and care of grandmas, aunties, sisters, mothers, daughters, nieces, caretakers, and friends in tribal lands, urban areas, and rural and remote geographic locations are also critical to reformation and change.

Native youths have their own wisdom to impart. The youth are our future, and they have strength in their own personal and public messages. At the National Congress of American Indian Youth Conference in 2018, they focused on the Indian Child Welfare Act. In a media release, they stated the following:

> The Indian Child Welfare Act was created in order to protect the best interest of Indian children and to promote the stability and security of tribal communities and families. We, as youth leaders, know that our identity is who we are, is within our culture, and within the tribal community that raises us. Our membership and blood quantum has never defined us as members of our tribal communities. To us, we are raised by tribal communities, because we learn not just from our family but from the communities as a whole. They teach us our languages, our traditions, they show us who we are as American Indian/Alaska Native youth; that is a right every American Indian/

Alaska Native child should have. They should not be taken from their tribal communities because when they are, a piece of our culture is lost. (National Congress of American Indian Youth, 2018)

This book began by exploring what healthy AI/AN children and families experience within a collectivistic orientation and then focused on pre-colonial experiences. AI/ANs come from honor-based systems that are grounded in respect for all things (e.g., humans, the land, nature, water, the spirit/relatives who have passed on). The etiology of well-being is found in the balance of a multiplicity of social, physical, socioecological, and spiritual relationships. The transmission of knowledge is based on teaching through stories, modeling, and apprenticeship. Restorative justice practices are critical in tribal communities.

The concept of child maltreatment was then discussed in the second chapter in the context of systemic and historical issues as well as systems embedded within the United States government. Then we discussed child maltreatment within public and private institutions, to which generations of Native children were exposed. We showed how systemic damage from the U.S. government had direct implications for AI/AN children and families. We covered the results of the boarding school era as well as contemporary AI/AN issues.

The third chapter was dedicated to exploring the interconnectedness of the Native child and family starting with the nested connection between the mind, body, and spirit with relational extensions to the cosmological and ecological realms. Then an examination of the protective factors, contextualized within an Indigenous lens, as well as effects/outcomes of child maltreatment occurred. These topics segued into the fourth chapter, which discussed aspects of institutional and systemic victimization and maltreatment, as well as highlighted policies, laws, and the implications for tribal communities. An extensive interweaving of the damage specific policies and laws have had on children, women, and families demonstrated the parallel effects these factors have had on Native lands. We implored you, the reader, to bear witness to the atrocities that are still happening to Native people (e.g., genocide, systemic oppression, sexual abuse, kidnapping, forced sterilization) in our U.S. society.

The fifth chapter examined best practices for intervening in cases of child maltreatment in AI/AN communities, including introducing a)

Indigenous prevention programs (federally funded), b) Native interventions, and c) adaptive treatment strategies (e.g., Honoring Children Mending the Circle, Bigfoot [2016]). Many of these Native-focused programs are sustained and have become community practices, regardless of grant funding. These models might suggest to future Native scholars, practitioners, advocates, and researchers that they consider implementing established efforts that are culturally and trauma-informed. In the sixth chapter, contemporary issues in child maltreatment advocacy and strategic ways advocates can become involved in addressing critical forms of child maltreatment were presented.

We now ask you to consider all the wisdom you are now holding. How will you address the call to action? How will you respond when you witness an injustice? Will you stand in solidarity and build bridges in an effort to liberate? Will you engage in reparations and reformation efforts? Will you reclaim your roots, honor your ancestors, and stand boldly in your entirety? What will you do?

Dr. B.M.J. Brayboy shared his thoughts on the need to reform the education system, as schools are not working for "a whole bunch of people who have particular sets and traits in common" (personal communication, March 10, 2021). Dr. Brayboy emphasized we need to think seriously about structures and systems. He stated, "If you've created the systems and structures, where there are people who don't fundamentally belong because of them . . . is that maltreatment? . . . It seems to me to be fundamentally abusive" (personal communication, March 10, 2021).

Dr. Brayboy, although speaking of education, expressed his thoughts about reformation in general too, extending his consideration to greater issues of systemic and institutional maltreatment. He indicated that if we designed a new set of structures, people would be allowed to thrive, which would be a foundational aspect; he would center on thriving and well-being for the individual and community (personal communication, March 10, 2021). He explained, "It's really about do we have family? Do we have connections to place? Are we sharing? Are we being good relatives? Are we in good relationship with folks around us? And if you're not, then there's a problem with a structure. . . . Generally speaking, structures help create these things and people adapt and adjust within them" (personal communication, March 10, 2021). His vision for a better future, inclusive of family, relationships, community, and structures, establishes a platform from where to begin, or rather, through an Indigenous lens, a return to traditional ideologies.

Future Directions

Recommendations for future directions of reform are in the areas of advocacy, practice, research, and capacity building through community. Many of the suggested areas are cost effective but require investments in time, sharing of knowledge and expertise, and commitment to the health and well-being of Native youth. These ideas for future directions are also straightforward and generally easy to implement; many rest in relationship building.

Advocacy

Advocacy requires active participation at many levels; change happens from the top down, bottom up, and in the middle where productiveness sometimes meet. In advocating for tribal communities, the communities themselves must define and identify their areas of strengths and needs. In the process of change, the areas of need should guide administrative, legislative, lobbyist, and public policy agendas; relationships with multidisciplinary allies should be cultivated; and data authorized for use by the tribal entity should be used strategically and as support for needed change (Willis et al., 2018). Too often, well-intentioned outside entities have missed the mark in speculation of tribal needs and misinterpretation of community dynamics.

Effective advocacy can also be generated through the synthesis of cross disciplinary issues. Thus, issues that have been presented in the contents of this book in need of reformation may benefit from the concerted efforts of psychology, education, law, and tribal entities. These efforts have gained momentum, such as with the Missing and Murdered Indigenous Peoples (MMIP) crisis, but more work must be done as it pertains to the Native child and family. Grassroot efforts and activism have been critical to issues such as MMIP and environmental exploitation, with people from many walks of life from different backgrounds working together.

In AI/AN communities and relationships, the conceptualization of advocacy also encompasses roles one may not necessarily consider part of the mainstream definition of advocacy. For many Native Peoples, the construct encumbers prayer and spirituality. Advocacy, through an Indigenous lens, highly correlates with ceremony, philanthropy, altruism, and sacrifice. Some of the most impoverished in the AI/AN population participate in the most sacred of ceremonies and possess some of the strongest prayers for the health and well-being of children, families, and communities. Many of those individuals that are homeless, challenged with medical and psychological health issues, and substance misuse, are those who either first-handedly experienced systemic, institutional, or governmental child maltreatment or are only one or two generations removed from those experiences.

Practice

In reading the material in the previous chapters, medical, mental health, child welfare, education, law, and mental health disciplines are called to action to change their approaches and practices. Given the carnage of historic and contemporary systems, institutions, and government treatment, the Native population merits equality and parity in mental and medical healthcare and healing practices. This effort also incites higher education and training of practitioners, paraprofessionals, educators, and professionals to embrace inclusivity and comprehensive materials that meet the unique needs of the AI/AN populations, instead of a one-size-fits-all mindset (refer to chapter 4 educational litigation) and archaic approaches to education. In addition, we advocate for a call to action for training and educational institutions to incorporate historical materials, literature, and articles authored by Native scholars. This would serve to significantly change the narrative taught to Native students and decrease educational racism, oppression, and maltreatment.

With regard to AI/AN children and families, there are several resources practitioners can use when planning clinical sessions. Mental health providers should consider implementing adapted treatments for the Native population such as Honoring Children (BigFoot & Schmidt, 2016), or relying on elements of Radical Healing (French et al., 2020) when developing treatment strategy. In addition, the Behavioral Health Services for American Indians and Alaska Natives—For Behavioral Health Service Providers, Administrators, and Supervisors, Treatment Improvement Protocol 61 (SAMHSA, 2018) may also be beneficial for providers to consult. The critical component will be seeking out supervision and consultation with Native para/professionals and/or culturally informed clinicians familiar with culturally salient approaches and culturally relevant clinical work. Supervisors and administrators engaging in cultural humility practices can appropriately support effective treatment and healing prevention, intervention, and postvention strategies for Native children and families. Educating oneself about Native history with the tribal population one works with, seeking culturally competent supervision, and using adaptive clinical components will transform therapeutic services, best supporting Native children, families, and communities.

Research

Given the work covered within the previous chapters, the examination of the historical and systemic impact of racism and oppression upon Native children and families is critical. Centering the experiences of Native children and families and working toward true egalitarian partnerships with tribal communities as research collaborators is ideal. Fully community-based participatory research (CBPR) is recommended for a multiplicity of reasons. Several of the main reasons for CBPR involve transparency, building relationships/partnerships, and trust; research has far too long not been beneficial for tribal nations. In a partnership based in CBPR, the outcomes of the research will benefit the tribal community.

From the start, tribal entities must determine the research question pursued in alliance with the scholarly researcher. In the exploration of the direction of the research, the researcher should identify the theoretical framework and measurement selection, fully explaining the methodologies and purpose to the tribal entity. At the onset of the research project, the use of data should be negotiated, as many tribes have invoked data sovereignty, since the data and outcomes belong to them. All of these considerations are imperative for meaningful research conducted with tribal children, families, and communities. As iterated, it is necessary to explore the needs of Native children and families within a cultural context when conducting research in any capacity.

Capacity Building through Community

The previous chapters reference centering our efforts on wellness, and one way to engage in this process is to provide mentorship and apprenticeship opportunities for Native youth. These types of prospects, formal and informal, provide opportunities to build relationships, hence strengthening individual and community interconnectedness and belongingness. In working with elders, the transmission of knowledge can be nurtured and developed into building community and sustainability. Tribal businesses can carve out scholarships, create programs focused on employment training, and develop other capacity building opportunities for Native youth. Tribal commerce may include, but is not limited to, artisans designing and creating cultural crafts; socioeconomic ventures in development corporation business areas; education department sponsored tutors, Head Start staff, or youth leadership roles; and tribal member enterprises such as in the culinary field specializing in Native foods. These types of opportunities not only center on capacity building but also contribute to furthering protective factors for Native youth.

Summary

Throughout the process of this book, mentors, elders, advisors, and highly revered scholars shared their heartfelt stories of growing up, personal experiences about their families, and about life. Our elders carry a plethora of wisdom and are willing to share if they are asked. But we must also listen. Dr. J. D. McDonald had some profound words, which will be used to close:

> As I continue my journey nowadays toward becoming an elder, I tell their stories. I feel compelled to enlighten folks with the elder's knowledge that this behavior is fundamentally wrong, nobody deserves to be hit, sexually assaulted, or bullied. Nobody! And most importantly that in Indian country, if we understand and respect our history, maybe we can strive to re-create the best parts of the "old days" and distance ourselves from the practice of hurting our relatives. I believe we can, but we have to face it first. What happened to us was not our fault, but what we do about it is our responsibility. (Personal communication, April 2, 2021)

We are all charged with the safety and responsibility of protecting our children. All children.

Recommended Readings
and Resources

Deloria, V., and D. R. Wildcat. 2001. *Power and Place: Indian Education in America*. Golden, CO: Fulcrum Publishing.

DiAngelo, R. 2018. *White Fragility: Why It's so Hard for White People to Talk about Racism*. Boston: Beacon Press.

Gallagher, H. G. 2001. *Etok: A Story of Eskimo Power*. Vandemere Press.

Grann, D. 2017. *Killers of the Flower Moon: The Osage Murders and the Birth of the FBI*. New York: Doubleday.

Hauman, E. S., and B.M.J. Brayboy. 2017. *Indigenous Innovations in Higher Education: Local Knowledge and Critical Research*. Rotterdam, Netherlands: Sense Publishers, 21–39.

Sando, J. S. (Eds.). 1992. *Pueblo Nations: Eight Centuries of Pueblo Indian History*, 1st ed. Santa Fe, NM: Clear Light Publishing.

Sarche, M. C., P. Spicer, P. Farrell, and H. E. Fitzgerald. 2011. *American Indian and Alaska Native Children and Mental Health: Development, Context, Prevention, and Treatment*. Westport, CT: Praeger/ABC-CLIO.

Warne, D. April 19, 2019. "Impact of Unresolved Trauma on American Indian Health Equity" Webinar from University of Washington School of Public Health. YouTube. https://www.youtube.com/watch?v=fS7WKxDtkwY.

References

Ashlynne Mike AMBER Alert in Indian Country Act, S.772, 115th Congress. (2017–2018). https://www.congress.gov/bill/115th-congress/senate-bill/772.

Association of American Indian Physicians. (2021). Strengthening our Native communities: How understanding adverse childhood experiences can help. https://www.aaip.org/programs/aces-toolkit/.

Bachman, R. (1992). *Death and violence on the reservation: Homicide, family violence, and suicide in American Indian populations.* Auburn House.

Balsamo, M., & Samuels, I. (2021, April 1). Justice Department working with tribes on missing persons. https://apnews.com/article/politics-missing-persons-native-americans-3a4b2ab1de1178f9eaf40ea8e1bd3ea9.

Barlow, A., Varipatis-Baker, E., Speakman, K., Ginsburg, G., Friberg, I., Goklish, N., Cowboy, B., Fields, P., Hastings, R., Pan, W., Reid, R., Santosham, M., & Walkup, J. (2006). Home-visiting intervention to improve child care among American Indian adolescent mothers: A randomized trial. *Archives of Pediatric Adolescent Medicine, 160*(11), 1101–1107.

Beals, J., Novins, D. K., Spicer, P., Whitesell, N. R., Mitchell, C. M., & Manson, S. M. (2006). Help seeking for substance use problems in two American Indian reservation populations. *Psychiatric Services, 57*(4), 512–520.

Beals, J., Novins, D. K., Whitesell, N. R., Spicer, P., Mitchell, C. M., & Manson, S. M. (2005). Prevalence of mental disorders and utilization of mental disorders and utilization of mental health services in two American Indian reservation populations: Mental health disparities in a national context. *American Journal of Psychiatry, 162*(9), 1723–1732.

Berkman, E. (2017, December 1). One size rarely fits all: How can we make psychological treatments more precise? *Psychology Today.* https://www.psychologytoday.com/us/blog/the-motivated-brain/201712/one-size-rarely-fits-all.

BigFoot, D. (2011). The process and dissemination of cultural adaptions of evidence-based practices for American Indian and Alaska Native children and their families. In M. C. Sarche, P. Spicer, P. Farrell, and H. E. Fitzgerald (Eds.), *American Indian and Alaska Native children and mental health: Developmental, context, prevention, and treatment* (pp. 285–307). Praeger/ABC-CLIO.

Bigfoot, D. S. (2020). Resilience in the face of trauma. *Prevention in Our Native American Communities, 1*(3), 10–14. https://pttcnetwork.org/sites/default/files/2020-07/Prev%20Vol%201%20Issue%203%20Summer%20 2020.pdf.

BigFoot, D. S., & Funderburk, B. W. (2011). Honoring children, making relatives: The cultural translation of parent-child interaction therapy for American Indian and Alaska Native Families. *Journal of Psychoactive Drugs, 43*(4), 309–318, https://doi: 10.1080/02791072.2011.628924.

BigFoot, D. S., & GreyWolf, I. (2014). Building resilience through Indigenous traditions: American Indian women gain strength through traditional practices. In Thema Bryant-Davis, Asuncion Miteria Austria, Debra M. Kawahara, Diane J. Willis (Eds.), *Religion and spirituality for diverse women: Foundations of strength and resilience* (pp. 3–17). Praeger.

BigFoot, D., & Schmidt, S. (2008). *Honoring Children, Mending the Circle* training manual. Oklahoma City: University of Oklahoma Health Sciences Center.

BigFoot, D. S., & Schmidt, S. R. (2012). American Indian and Alaska Native children: Honoring Children Mending the Circle. In J. Cohen, A. Mannarino & E. Deblinger (Eds.), *Trauma-focused CBT for children and adolescents* (pp. 280–300). Guilford Press.

Blue Bird Jernigan, V., Huyser, K. R., Valdes, J., & Watts Simonds, V. (2017). Food insecurity among American Indians and Alaska Natives: A national profile using the current population survey-food security supplement. *Journal of Hunger & Environmental Nutrition, 12*(1), 1–10. https://doi: 10.1080/19320248.2016.1227750.

Blume, A. K., Tehee, M., & Galliher, R. V. (2019). Experiences of discrimination and prejudice among American Indian youth: Links to psychosocial functioning. In *Handbook of Children and Prejudice* (pp. 389–404). Springer.

Bowman, P., & Howard, C. (1985). Race-related socialization, motivation, and academic achievement: A study of Black youths in three-generation families. *Journal of the American Academy of Child Psychiatry, 24*(2), 134–141.

Brave Heart, M. Y., & DeBruyn, L. M. (1998). The American Indian holocaust: Healing historical unresolved grief. *American Indian and Alaska Native Mental Health Research, 8*(2), 56–78. https://pubmed.ncbi.nlm.nih.gov/9842066/.

Brayboy, B.M.J. (2005). Toward a tribal critical race theory in education. *The Urban Review, 37*(5), 425–446.

Brayboy, B.M.J., & Chin, J. (2020). On the development of terrortory. *Contexts, 19*(3), 22–27.

Brockie, T. N., Heinzelmann, M., & Gill, J. (2013). A framework to examine the role of epigenetics in health disparities among Native Americans. *Nursing Research and Practice*, 1–9. https://doi.org/10.1155/2013/410395.

Bureau of Indian Affairs. (n.d.). Tribal court systems. https://www.bia.gov /CFRCourts/tribal-justice-support-directorate.

Burke Lefever, J. E., Bigelow, K. M., Carta, J. J., Borkowski, J. G., Grandfield, E., McCune, L., Irvin, D. W., & Warren, S. F. (2017). Long-term impact of a cell phone-enhanced parenting intervention. *Child Maltreatment, 22*(4), 305–314. https://doi.org/10.1177/1077559517723125.

Burrage, R. (2018). Trauma, loss, resilience, and resistance in the Beauval Indian Residential School. *Theses and Dissertations*. https://hdl.handle .net/2027.42/14590.

Cajete, G. (2016). *Native science: Natural laws of interdependence*. Clear Light Publishers.

Campbell, C. D., & Evans-Campbell, T. (2011). Historical trauma and Native American child development and mental health: An overview. In M. C. Sarche, P. Spicer, P. Farrell, and H. E. Fitzgerald (Eds.), *American Indian and Alaska Native children and mental health: Development, context, prevention, and treatment* (pp. 1–26). Praeger/ABC-CLIO.

Campbell, L. (2018). *Language isolates*. Taylor & Francis.

Carlisle Indian School Digital Resource Center. (n.d.). Cemetery Information. http://carlisleindian.dickinson.edu/cemetery-information.

Center for American Indian Health. (n.d.). Family Spirit Home Visiting Program. https://caih.jhu.edu.

Chaffin, M., Bard, D., BigFoot, D. S., & Maher, E. J. (2012). Is a structured, manualized, evidence-based treatment protocol culturally competent and equivalently effective among American Indian parents in child welfare? *Child Maltreatment, 17*(3), 242–252. https://doi.org/10.1177 /1077559512457239.

Chaney, C. (2018). Data sovereignty and the tribal law and order act. *The federal lawyer*. https://static1.squarespace.com/static/5d3799de845 604000199cd24/t/5d73f6d44b1c8730fdea0275/1567880916590 /Data+Sovereignty+and+Tribal+Law.pdf.

Chiedi, J. A. (2019). Indian health service has strengthened patient protection policies but must fully integrate them into practice and organizational culture. *U.S. Department of Health and Human Services Office of Inspector General Report*. https://oig.hhs.gov/oei/reports/oei-06-19 -00330.pdf.

Child Welfare Information Gateway. (n.d.). *SafeCare*. https://www .childwelfare.gov/topics/preventing/prevention-programs/homevisit /homevisitprog/safe-care/

Clark, J. F. (2021). Help for missing American Indian and Alaska Native children. *Department of Justice Journal of Federal Law and Practice, 69*(1), 5–20.

Cooper, M. (1999). *Indian school: Teaching the White man's way*. Clarion Books.

Cornell, S., & Kalt, J. P. (2010). American Indian self-determination: The political economy of a successful policy. Joint Occasional Papers on Native Affairs, Native Nations Institute. https://nni.arizona.edu/pubs /jopna-wp1_cornell&kalt.pdf.

Crofoot, T. L., & Harris, M. S. (2012). An Indian child welfare perspective on disproportionality in child welfare. *Children and Youth Services Review*, *34*(9), 1667–1674.

Crofoot Graham, T. L. (2002). Using reasons for living to connect to American Indian healing traditions. *Journal of Sociology & Social Welfare*, *29*(1), Article 5, 55–75. https://scholarworks.wmich.edu/jssw /vol29/iss1/5.

Cross, T. [National Indian Child Welfare Association] (2020, November 17). Touchstones of hope dialogue series: Introduction. [Webinar]. YouTube. https://www.youtube.com/watch?v=bSoKIlOVhmk&feature =youtu.be.

Cross, T. L. (2020). Racial disproportionality and disparities among American Indian and Alaska Native populations. In: A. J. Dettlaff (Ed.), *Racial disproportionality and disparities in the child welfare system: Child maltreatment*. Contemporary Issues in Research and Policy, vol. 11 (pp. 99–125). Springer, Cham. https://doi.org/10.1007/978-3-030-54314-3 _6.

Crystal, D. (1997). *The Cambridge encyclopedia of language* (vol. 2). Cambridge University Press.

Cunningham, J. K., Solomon, T. A., & Muramoto, M. L. (2016). Alcohol use among Native Americans compared to Whites: Examining the veracity of the "Native American elevated alcohol consumption" belief. *Drug and Alcohol Dependence*, *160*, 65–75. https://doi.org/10.1016/j .drugalcdep.2015.12.015.

Curran, T. (Producer). (2011, April 11). *The silence* (Season 2011, Episode 12) [TV Series Episode]. In *Frontline*. PBS. https://www.pbs.org/wgbh /pages/frontline/the-silence/.

Daines, M. (2017). Statement of Senator Mark Daines on the Senate Floor [citing Missing and Murdered Native Women and Girls statistics]. Washington, DC. https://www.daines.senate.gov/news/videos/watch /daines-to-mark-national-day-of-awareness-for-missing-and-murdered -native-women-and-girls.

Daniel, R. (2020). Since you asked: What data exists about Native American people in the criminal justice system? Prison Policy Initiative. https:// www.prisonpolicy.org/blog/2020/04/22/native/.

Davidson, V.N.D. (2018). Changing the narrative: In-state of Alaska Department of Health and Social Services (Ed.), Cultural Resources for Alaska Families (p.7). https://dhss.alaska.gov/ocs/Documents/Cultural ResourcesGuide.pdf.

DeAngelis, T. (2009). Unmasking "racial micro aggressions." *Monitor on Psychology, 40*(2), 42. https://www.apa.org/monitor/2009/02 /microaggression.

Deer, S. (2017). Bystander no more? Improving the federal response to sexual violence in Indian country. *Utah Law Review*, 771–800. https://dc.law .utah.edu/ulr/vol2017/iss4/7/.

Deer, S. (2019). (En)gendering Indian law: Indigenous feminist legal theory in the United States. *Yale Journal of Law and Feminism, 31,* 1–34. https://openyls.law.yale.edu/bitstream/handle/20.500.13051/7123/En _Gendering_Indian_Law_Indigenous_Feminist_Legal_Theory_in _the_United.pdf?sequence=2.

Delaney, T., & Thompson, D. L. (2020, October 5). How Nonprofits can stop Trump's effort to roll back diversity training. *Nonprofit Quarterly.* https://nonprofitquarterly.org/how-nonprofits-can-stop-trumps-effort -to-roll-back-diversity-training/.

Deloria, V., & Lytle, C. M. (1983). *American Indians, American justice.* University of Texas Press.

Deloria, V., & Wildcat, D. R. (2001). *Power and place: Indian education in America.* Fulcrum Publishing.

Demmert, W. G. (2001). A review of the research literature: Improving academic performance among Native American students. ERIC Clearinghouse on Rural Education and Small Schools. https://files.eric .ed.gov/fulltext/ED463917.pdf.

Demmert, W. G. (2011). Culturally based education: Promoting academic success and the general well-being of Native American students. In M. C. Sarche, P. Spicer, P. Farrell, & H. E. Fitzgerald (Eds.), *American Indian and Alaska Native children and mental health: Developmental, context, prevention, and treatment* (pp. 255–267). Praeger.

DiAngelo, R. (2018). *White fragility: Why it's so hard for White people to talk about racism.* Beacon Press.

Duran, E. (2006). *Healing the soul wound: Counseling with American Indians and other Native peoples.* Teachers College Press.

Duran, E., & Duran, B. (1995). *Native American postcolonial psychology.* State University of New York Press.

Duran, E., Firehammer, J., & Gonzalez, J. (2008). Liberation psychology as the path toward healing cultural soul wounds. *Journal of Counseling and Development, 86*(3), 288–295.

EchoHawk, L. (2001). Child sexual abuse in Indian Country: Is the guardian keeping in mind the seventh generation? *N.Y.U. Journal of Legislation & Public Policy, 5.* https://heinonline.org/HOL/Landing Page?handle=hein.journals/nyulpp5&div=14&id=&page.

Evans-Campbell, T. (2008). Historical trauma in American Indian/Native Alaska communities: A multilevel framework for exploring impacts on individuals, families, and communities. *Journal of Interpersonal Violence, 23*(3), 316–338. https://pubmed.ncbi.nlm.nih.gov/18245571/.

Felitti, V. J., Anda, R. F., Nordenberg, D., Williamson, D. F., Spitz, A. M., Edwards, V., & Marks, J. S. (1998). Relationship of childhood abuse and household dysfunction to many of the leading causes of death in adults: The Adverse Childhood Experiences (ACE) Study. *American Journal of Preventive Medicine, 14*(4), 245–258.

Finkelman, P., & Garrison, T. A. (2009). Indian Self-Determination and Education Assistance Act (ISDEAA; 1975). (Eds.) *Encyclopedia of United States Indian policy and law* (pp. 434–435). CQ Press. https://dx.doi.org /10.4135/9781604265767.n317.

Fish, J., Livingston, J. A., VanZile-Tamsen, C., & Wolf, D.A.P.S. (2017). Victimization and substance use among Native American college students. *Journal of College Student Development, 58*(3), 413–431.

French, B. H., Lewis, J. A., Mosley, D. V., Adames, H. Y., Chavez-Duenas, N. Y., Chen, G. A., & Neville, H. A. (2020). Toward a psychological framework of radical healing in communities of color. *The Counseling Psychologist, 48*(1), 14–26. https://journals.sagepub.com/doi/full/10.1177 /0011000019843506.

Funderburk, B. W., Gurwitch, R., & BigFoot, D. S. (2005). Honoring children, making relatives (Parent child interaction therapy training manual). Indian Country Child Trauma Center, University of Oklahoma Health Sciences Center.

Furlow, B. (2020, August 22). Federal investigation finds hospital violated patients' rights by profiling, separating Native mothers and newborns. *Propublica.* https://www.propublica.org/article/federal-investigation -finds-hospital-violated-patients-rights-by-profiling-separating-native -mothers-and-newborns.

Gallagher, H. G. (2001). *Etok: A story of Eskimo power.* Vandemere Press.

Garrett, J. T., & Garrett, M. W. (1994). The path of good medicine: Understanding and counseling Native American Indians. *Journal of Multicultural Counseling and Development, 22*(3), 134–144.

Garrett, M. T., Garrett, J. T., Torres-Rivera, E., Wilbur, M., & Roberts-Wilbur, J. (2005). Laughing it up: Native American humor as spiritual tradition. *Journal of Multicultural Counseling and Development, 33*(4), 194–204. https://doi.org/10.1002/j.2161-1912.2005.tb00016.x.

Garrett, M. T., & Pichette, E. F. (2000). Red as an apple: Native American acculturation and counseling with or without reservation. *Journal of Counseling & Development, 78*(1), 3–13. https://doi.org/10.1002/j.1556 -6676.2000.tb02554.x.

Garth, T. R. (1927). A comparison of mental abilities of nomadic and sedentary Indians on a basis of education. *American Anthropologist, 29*(3), 206–213. http://www.jstor.org/stable/661146.

Gershater-Molko, R. M., Lutzker, J. R., & Wesch, D. (2002). Using recidivism to evaluate project SafeCare: Teaching bonding, safety, and health care skills to parents. *Child Maltreatment, 7*(3), 277–285. https://doi.org/10.1177/1077559502007003009.

Gone, J. P. (2008). 'So I can be like a Whiteman': The cultural psychology of space and place in American Indian mental health. *Culture & Psychology, 14*(3), 369–399. https://doi.org/10.1177/1354067X08092639.

Gone, J. P. (2011). Is psychological science a-cultural? *Cultural Diversity and Ethnic Minority Psychology, 17*(3), 234–242. https://doi.org/10.1037/a0023805.

Gone, J. P. (2019). "The thing happened as he wished": Recovering an American Indian cultural psychology. *American Journal of Community Psychology, 64*(1–2), 172–184. https://doi.org/10.1002/ajcp.12353.

Gone, J. P., & Kirmayer, L. J. (2020). Advancing Indigenous mental health research: Ethical, conceptual and methodological challenges. *Journal of Transcultural Psychiatry, 57*(2), 235–249. https://doi.org/10.1177/1363461520923151.

Goodkind, J. R., Gorman, B., Hess, J. M., Parker, D. P., & Hough, R. L. (2015). Reconsidering culturally competent approaches to American Indian healing and well-being. *Qualitative Health Research, 25*(4), 486–499. https://doi.org/10.1177/1049732314551056.

Goodluck, C., & Willeto, A.A.A. (2009). Seeing the protective rainbow: How families survive and thrive in the American Indian and Alaska Native Community. Annie E. Casey Foundation.

Gordon, H.S.J., & Roberts, T.W.M. (2021). Missing or murdered Indigenous people: Culturally based prevention strategies. *Department of Justice Journal of Federal Law and Practice, 69*(1), 47–70.

Gourneau, J. L. (2002). Development of the American Indian biculturalism inventory—Northern Plains. *Theses and Dissertations.* 1059. https://commons.und.edu/theses/1059.

Greenfield, B. L., Venner, K. L., Tonigan, J. S., Honeyestewa, M., Hubbell, H., & Bluehorse, D. (2018). Low rates of alcohol and tobacco use, strong cultural ties for Native American college students in the Southwest. *Addictive Behaviors, 82*, 122–128. https://doi.org/10.1016/j.addbeh.2018.02.032.

GreyWolf, I. (2018, October 8). Don't take it personally—Really. Psychology benefits society. https://psychologybenefits.org/2018/10/08/how-psychologists-can-contribute-to-reconciliation-with-indigenous-peoples-of-united-states/.

Gutierrez, R. A. (1991). *When Jesus came, the corn mothers went away: Marriage, sexuality, and power in New Mexico, 1500–1846.* Stanford University Press.

Haldane, F. B. (1986). In A. J. McClanahan (Ed.), *Our stories, Our lives* (pp. 140–154), The CIRI Foundation.

Hensley (Iggiagruk), W. L. (2009). *Fifty miles from tomorrow: A memoir of Alaska and the real people.* Farrar, Strauss and Giroux.

Hill, J. S., Pace, T. M., & Robbins, R. R. (2010). Decolonizing personality assessment and honoring Indigenous voices: A critical examination of the MMPI-2. *Cultural Diversity and Ethnic Minority Psychology, 16*(1), 16–25. https://doi.org/10.1037/a0016110.

Hilleary, C. (2018, September 27). For Native American clergy sex abuse survivors, justice is elusive. *Voice of America.* https://www.voanews.com /a/native-americans-forgotten-survivors-of-clergy-abuse-church-coverup /4589535.html.

Hodge, D. R., & Limb, G. E. (2010). A Native American perspective on spiritual assessment: The strengths and limitations of a complementary set of assessment tools. *Health & Social Work, 35*(2), 121–131.

Hopkins, K. (2019, July 26). Clergy abused an entire generation in this village: With new traumas, justice remains elusive. Propublica. https:// www.propublica.org/article/stebbins-st-michael-alaska-clergy-abused-an -entire-generation-with-new-traumas-justice-remains-elusive.

Hudetz, M. (2018, May 13). Teens' experience shows campus reality for Native Americans. *Associated Press.* https://apnews.com/article/0189d98 791824d4c90945fca5494a15e.

Isaac, G., Finn, S., Joe, J. R., Hoover, E., Gone, J. P., Lefthand-Begay, C., & Hill, S. (2018). Native American perspectives on health and traditional ecological knowledge. *Environmental Health Perspectives, 126*(12), 1–10. https://ehp.niehs.nih.gov/doi/pdf/10.1289/EHP1944.

Isaacs, D. S., Tehee, M., Green, J., Straits, K.J.E., & Ellington, T. (2020). When psychologists take a stand: Barriers to trauma response services and advocacy for American Indian communities. *Journal of Trauma & Dissociation, 21*(4), 468–483.

Jiron, R. (2016, December 21). *Randy Jiron.* Humans of New Mexico. Center of Southwest Culture. https://humansofnewmexico.com/2016/12/21 /randy-jiron/

Johnson, G., Weaver, C., & Frosch, D. (Producers). (2019, February 12). *Predator on the reservation* (Season 2019, Episode 7) [TV Series Episode], In *Frontline.* PBS. https://www.pbs.org/wgbh/frontline/film/predator -on-the-reservation/.

Johnston-Goodstar, K., & VeLure Roholt, R. (2017). "Our kids aren't dropping out; they're being pushed out": Native American students and racial microaggressions in schools. *Journal of Ethnic & Cultural Diversity in Social Work: Innovation in Theory, Research & Practice, 26*(1–2), 30–47. https://doi.org/10.1080/15313204.2016.1263818.

Kastelic, S. L. (2013, December 9). American Indian/Alaska Native children exposed to violence in the home. National Indian Child Welfare Association. https://www.nicwa.org/wp-content/uploads/2016/11/NICWATesti monyTaskForceonAIANChildrenExposedtoViolence_Dec2013.pdf.

Kawagley, A. O. (2006). *A Yupiaq worldview: A pathway to ecology and spirit.* Waveland Press, Inc.

Kemberling, M. M., & Avellaneda-Cruz, L. D. (2013). *Healthy Native families: Preventing violence at all ages* (2nd ed.). Alaska Native Tribal Health Consortium, Alaska Native Epidemiology Center.

Kirmayer, L. J., Gone, J. P., & Moses, J. (2014). Rethinking historical trauma. *Transcultural Psychiatry, 51*(3), 299–319. https://doi.org/10.1177/1363461514536358.

Kunesh, P. H. (2007). Banishment as cultural justice in contemporary tribal legal systems. *New Mexico Law Review, 37*(1), 85–145. https://digital repository.unm.edu/cgi/viewcontent.cgi?article=1222&context=nmlr.

LaFortune, K. A., & Rush, V. S. (2019). A call to study Native Americans' experiences in tribal and U.S. courts. *American Psychological Association Monitor on Psychology, 4*(50), 29.

LaRocque, A. R., McDonald, J. D., Weatherly, J. N., & Ferraro, F. R. (2011). Indian sports nicknames/logos: Affective difference between American Indian and non-Indian college students. *American Indian and Alaska Native Mental Health Research, 18*(2), 1–16.

Lawrence, J. (2000). The Indian Health Service and the sterilization of Native American women. *American Indian Quarterly, 24*(3), 400–419. https://doi.org/10.1353/aiq.2000.0008.

Lawrence, J. A. (1999). *Indian Health Service: Sterilization of Native American women, 1960s–1970s* [Doctoral dissertation, Oklahoma State University].

Limb, G. E., Chance, T., & Brown, E. F. (2004). An empirical examination of the Indian Child Welfare Act and its impact on cultural and familial preservation for American Indian children. *Child Abuse & Neglect, 28*(12), 1279–1289. https://doi.org/10.1016/j.chiabu.2004.06.01.2

Lincourt, T., Ross, R. J., & McCloskey, C. (2021, April). Restorative justice in Indian Country. *Public Service Newsletter, Psychologists in Public Service, APA Division 18.* https://www.apadivisions.org/division-18/publications/newsletters/public-service/2021/04/justice.

Lomawaima, K. T. (2018). Indian boarding schools, before and after: A personal introduction. *Journal of American Indian Education, 57*(1), 11–21.

LPC Consulting Associates, Inc. (2013). Birth & beyond home visiting program: Nurturing parenting program child protective services outcomes report. *Executive Summary July 2010-June 2013.* https://www.nurturingparenting.com/images/cmsfiles/cpsoutcomesreport2010-2013final112520132.pdf.

Luker, T. (2000). The coercive sterilization of Native American women by the Indian Health Services (1970–1974). *The Alexandrian, 3*(1), 40–71. https://journals.troy.edu/index.php/test/article/view/365.

Lyons, S. R. (2000). Rhetorical sovereignty: What do American Indians want from writing? *College Composition and Communication, 51*(3), 447–468. https://doi.org/10.2307/358744.

Mail, P. D., Conner, J., & Conner, C. N. (2006.) New collaborations with Native Americans in the conduct of community research. *Health Education & Behavior, 33*(2): 148–153. https://doi.org/10.1177/1090198104272054.

Males, M. (2014, August 26). *Who are police killing?* Center on Juvenile and Criminal Justice. http://www.cjcj.org/news/8113.

Martell, L., McDonald, J. D., Barragan, B., Ziegler, S., & Williams, V. (2020). Examining cultural identification and alcohol use among American Indian and Caucasian college students. *American Indian & Alaska Native Mental Health Research: The Journal of the National Center, 27*(2), 23–36. https://doi.org/10.5820/aian.2702.2020.23.

Matamonasa-Bennett, A. (2015). "A disease of the outside people": Native American men's perceptions of intimate partner violence. *Psychology of Women Quarterly, 39*(1), 20–36. https://doi.org/10.1177/0361684314543783.

Matamonasa-Bennett, A. (2017). "The poison that ruined the nation": Native American men-alcohol, identity, and traditional healing. *American Journal of Men's Health, 11*(4), 1142–1154. https://doi.org/10.1177/1557988315576937.

May, A. (1995). The epidemiology of alcohol abuse among American Indians: The mythical and real properties. *The IHS Primary Care Provider, 20*(3), 49–56. https://nativehealthdatabase.net/digital-heritage/epidemiology-alcohol-abuse-among-american-indians-mythical-and-real-properties.

May, P. A. (1995). The prevention of alcohol and other substance abuse among American Indians: A review and analysis of the literature. In P. Langston (Ed.), *The challenge for participating research in the prevention of alcohol-related problems in ethnic communities.* Washington, DC: National Institute on Alcohol Abuse and Alcoholism and Center for Substance Abuse Prevention.

McBride, R. [KTVA News]. (2020, January 31). Elsie Boudreau speaks at 2019 Rural Providers Conference [Video]. YouTube. https://www.youtube.com/watch?v=5v5hSQeNI6U.

McDonald, J. D., & Chaney, J. (2003). Resistance to multiculturalism: The "Indian problem." In J. S. Mio & G. Y. Iwamasa (Eds.), *Culturally diverse mental health the challenges of research and resistance* (pp. 39–54*).* Brunner-Routledge.

McDonald, J. D., Gonzalez, J., & Sargent, E. (2019). Cognitive behavior therapy with American Indians. In G. Y. Iwamasa & P. A. Hays (Eds.), *Culturally responsive cognitive behavior therapy: Practice and supervision* (pp. 27–51). American Psychological Association. https://doi.org/10.1037/0000119-002.

McDonald, J. D., Morton, R., & Stewart, C. (1993). Clinical concerns with American Indian patients. *Innovations in Clinical Practice: A Source Book, 12*, 437–454.

McDonald, J. D., Ross, R. J., Kilwein, T. M., & Sargent, E. (2018). Cognitive behavior therapy for depression with American Indians. In Chang, E. C., Downey, C. A., Hirsch, J. K., & Yu, E. A. (Eds.), *Cognitive-behavioral models, measures, and treatments for depression, anxiety, and stress in ethnic and racial groups.* American Psychological Association.

McDonald, J. D., Ross, R., & Rose, W. (2016, August). The American Indian biculturalism inventory—Northern Plains. [Poster presentation]. American Psychological Association, Denver, CO.

Meriam, L., Brown, R. A., Cloud, H. R., Dale, E. E., Duke, E., Edwards, H. R, McKenzie, F. A., Mark, M. A., Ryan, W. C., & Spillman., W. J. (1928). *The problems of Indian administration.* John Hopkins Press. https://files.eric.ed.gov/fulltext/ED087573.pdf.

Minthorn, R. Z. (2018). Indigenous motherhood in the academy, building our children to be good relatives. *Wicazo Sa Review, 33*(2), 62–75. https://www.muse.jhu.edu/article/780062.

Mirsky, L. (2004, April 27). Restorative justice practices of Native American, first nation and other indigenous people of North America: Part one. International Institute for Restorative Practices. https://www.iirp.edu/pdf/natjust1.pdf.

Mokdad, A. H., Marks, J. S., Stroup, D. F., & Gerberding, J. L. (2004). Actual causes of death in the United States, 2000. *Journal of the American Medical Association, 291*(10), 1238–1245. https://doi.org/10.1001/jama.291.10.1238.

Moorehead, V. D., Gone, J. P., & December, D. (2015). A gathering of Native American healers: Exploring the interface of indigenous tradition and professional practice. *American Journal of Community Psychology, 56*(3), 383–394. https://pubmed.ncbi.nlm.nih.gov/26351006/.

Morsette, A., Swaney, G., Stolle, D., Schuldberg, D., van den Pol, R., & Young, M. (2009). Cognitive behavioral intervention for trauma in schools (CBITS): School-based treatment on a rural American Indian reservation. *Journal of Behavior Therapy and Experimental Psychiatry, 40*(1), 169–178. https://doi.org/10.1016/j.jbtep.2008.07.006.

Napoleon, H. (1991). *Yuuyaraq: The way of the human being.* Center for Cross-Cultural Studies, College of Rural Alaska.

Naranjo, T. (2017). Stories of place and intergenerational learning. In E. S. Hauman & B. McK. J. Brayboy (Eds.), *Indigenous innovations in higher education local knowledge and critical research* (pp. 21–39). Sense Publishers.

National Center for Healthy Safe Children. (n.d.). Grantee Programs. https://healthysafechildren.org/grantee.

National Conference of State Legislatures. (2020, September 28). *Disproportionality and Disparity in Child Welfare.* https://www.ncsl.org/research/human-services/disproportionality-and-disparity-in-child-welfare.aspx.

National Congress of American Indians. (2018). NCAI Youth Commission. In the news. https://www.ncai.org/native-youth/ncai-youth-commission/news.

National Congress of American Indians. (2021a). *About Native youth.* https://www.ncai.org/native-youth/about.

National Congress of American Indians. (2021b). Demographics. https://www.ncai.org/about-tribes/demographics.

National Congress of American Indians Research Policy Center. (2021). A First Look at the 2020 Census American Indian/Alaska Native Redistricting Data. https://www.ncai.org/policy-research-center/research-data/prc -publications/Overview_of_2020_AIAN_Redistricting_Data_FINAL _8_13_2021.pdf

National Congress of American Indian Youth Commission. (2018). In the news. https://www.ncai.org/native-youth/ncai-youth-commission/news.

National Crime Information Center. (2019). Missing person and unidentified person statistics pursuant to the requirements of the crime control act of 1990, Pub. L No. 1010–647, 104 Stat. 4789.

National Indian Child Welfare Association. (2007). *Positive Indian parenting*. National Indian Child Welfare Association.

National Indian Child Welfare Association. (2015, September). Setting the record straight: The Child Welfare Act fact sheet. https://www.nicwa .org/wp-content/uploads/2017/04/Setting-the-Record-Straight-ICWA -Fact-Sheet.pdf.

National Indian Child Welfare Association. (2016). *Positive Indian parenting*. National Indian Child Welfare Association.

National Indian Child Welfare Association. (2021). *About ICWA*. https:// www.nicwa.org/about-icwa/

National Indian Child Welfare Association. (2021). Reconciliation in Child Welfare Touchstones of Hope Dialogue Series. https://www.nicwa.org /touchstones-of-hope-dialogues/.

National Network to Eliminate Disparities in Behavioral Health (2022). Project Venture. NEED. https://nned.net/?s=Project+Venture.

National vs. Native Missing Youth Statistics, AMBER Alert-Indian Country. (2017). https://amber-ic.org/wpcontent/uploads/2017/11/ NationalvsNativeMissing Youth.pdf.

Neblett, Jr., E.W., Rivas-Drake, D., & Umana-Taylor, A. J. (2012). The promise of racial and ethnic protective factors in promoting ethnic minority youth development. *Child Development Perspectives*, *6*(3), 295–303. https://doi.org/10.1111/j.1750-8606.2012.00239.x.

Nelson, S. H., & Manson, S. M. (2000). Mental health and mental disorders. In E. R. Rhoades (Ed.), *American Indian health innovations in health care, promotion, and policy* (pp. 3–18). Johns Hopkins University Press.

Norris, T., Vines, P. L., & Hoeffel, E. M. (2012). The American Indian and Alaska Native population: 2010. U.S. Census. https://www.census.gov /library/publications/2012/dec/c2010br-10.html.

Oetting, E. R., & Beauvais, F. (1991). Orthogonal cultural identification theory: The cultural identification of minority adolescents. *International Journal of the Addictions*, *25*(sup5), 655–685. https://doi.org/10.3109 /10826089109077265.

Office of Juvenile Justice and Delinquency Prevention. (2017). National vs. Native missing youth statistics: AMBER Alerts in Indian Country fact

sheet. https://ojjdp.ojp.gov/publications/national-vs-native-missing
-youth-statistics.pdf.

Palmiste, C. (2011). From the Indian adoption project to the Indian child
welfare act: The resistance of Native American communities. *Indigenous Policy Journal, 22*(1), 1–10. https://www.academia.edu/31141445
/From_the_Indian_Adoption_Project_to_the_Indian_Child
_Welfare_Act.

Pecos, R. (2020). The gift of language from one Pueblo perspective.
In R. B. Martinez & M. J. H. Lopez (Eds.), *The shoulders we stand on:
A history of bilingual education in New Mexico* (pp. 13–24). University
of New Mexico Press.

Pember, M. A. (2016). *Intergenerational trauma: Understanding Natives'
inherited pain.* Indian Country Today Media Network. http://www
.mapember.com/ICMN-All-About-Generations-Trauma.pdf.

Peterson, C., Florence, C., & Klevens, J. (2018). The economic burden of
child maltreatment in the United States, 2015. *Child Abuse & Neglect, 86,*
178–183. https://doi.org/10.1016/j.chiabu.2018.09.018.

Pewewardy, C. (2002). Learning styles of American Indian/Alaska Native
students: A review of the literature and implications for practice. *Journal
of American Indian Education, 41*(3), 22–56. http://www.jstor.org/stable
/24398583.

Pomerville, A., Burrage, R. L., & Gone, J. P. (2016). Empirical findings from
psychotherapy research with indigenous populations: A systematic
review. *Journal of Consulting and Clinical Psychology, 84*(12), 1023–1038.
https://doi.org/10.1037/ccp0000150.

Popick, J. (2006). Native American women, past, present, and future.
Lethbridge Undergraduate Research Journal,1(1), 1–8. https://opus.uleth
.ca/handle/10133/462.

Prairie Chicken, M. L. (2019*). Coping styles as mediators between American
Indian cultural identification and life satisfaction* (2480). [Thesis,
University of North Dakota]. *Theses and Dissertations.* https://commons
.und.edu/theses/2480.

Preucel, R., & Pecos, R. (2015). Cochiti Pueblo, core values, and authorized
heritage discourse. In K. L. Samuels & T. Rico, *Heritage keywords:
Rhetoric and redescription in cultural heritage* (pp. 221–242). University
Press of Colorado. https://www.academia.edu/14443783/Place_Cochiti
_Pueblo_Core_Values_and_Authorized_Heritage_Discourse.

Public Counsel. (2020, October 2). Historic settlement reached in advancing the educational rights of Native American students [Press Release].
https://law.stanford.edu/wp-content/uploads/2020/11/Historic
-Settlement-Reached-In-Advancing-The-Educational-Rights-Of-Native
-American-Students-Press-Releases-Public-Counsel-2Oct2020.pdf.

Pueblo of Laguna. (2020, October 12). Title VII—Children, families and
elderly. Chapter 1: Children. https://library.municode.com/nm/pueblo
_of_laguna/codes/tribal_code?nodeId=TITVIICHFAEL.

Quandelacy, T. (2010). Nuclear racism: Uranium mining on the Laguna and Navajo reservations. *Interdisciplinary Journal of Health, Ethics, and Policy, 6–9.* http://s3.amazonaws.com/tuftscope_articles/documents /52/6.0_Nuclear_Racism_Uranium_Mining_on_the_Laguna.pdf.

Rameriz, I. (2020, September 14). An ICE nurse revealed that a Georgia detention center is performing mass hysterectomies. *Yahoo! Life.* https://www.yahoo.com/lifestyle/ice-nurse-revealed-georgia-detention -215816246.html.

Ramos, K., Kauahi, K., Estrellado, J., Green, J., & Celestial, J. E. (in press). Chapter 6: Treatment Planning. In J. Estrellado, J. E. Celestial, & L. Felipe (Eds.), *Clinical interventions for internalized oppression.* Cognella.

Redvers, N., & Blondin, B. (2020). Traditional Indigenous medicine in North America: A scoping review. *PloS ONE, 15*(8), 1–21. https://doi.org /10.1371/journal.pone.0237531

Rennie, L., Davila, S., Keller, J., Friedl, S., & Strickland, A. (2021, January 25). Supporting administrative actions taken by newly-inaugurated Biden administration. *American Psychological Association Services, Inc.* https://www.apaservices.org/advocacy/news/biden-executive-orders

Robbins, C. C. (1999). Pueblo Indians receive remains of ancestors. *New York Times.* http://www.nytimes.com/1999/05/23/us/pueblo-indians -receive-remains-of-ancestors.html.

Rolnick, A. C. (2016). Untangling the Web: Juvenile justice in Indian Country. *NYUJ Legislation & Public Policy, 19*(49), 49–140. https:// www.nyujlpp.org/wp-content/uploads/2016/05/Rolnick-Juvenile-Justice -in-Indian-Country-19nyujlpp49.pdf.

Romero, M. E. (1994). Identifying giftedness among Keresan Pueblo Indians: The Keres study. *Journal of the American Indian, 34*(1), 35–58. https://www.jstor.org/stable/24398400.

Romero-Little, M. E. (2011). Learning the community's curriculum: The linguistic, social, and cultural resources of American Indian and Alaska Native children. In M. C. Sarche, P. Spicer, P. Farrell, & H. E. Fitzgerald (Eds.), *American Indian and Alaska Native children and mental health: Development, context, prevention, and treatment* (pp. 89–99). Praeger/ ABC-CLIO, LLC. https://psycnet.apa.org/record/2011-23063-005.

Romero-Little, E., Sims, C., & Romero, A. (2014). Revisiting the Keres study to envision the future. In D. Paris & M. T. Winn (Eds.), *Humanizing research: Decolonizing qualitative inquiry with youth and communities* (pp. 161–174). Sage Publications, Inc.

Rosay, A. B. (2016). *Violence against American Indian and Alaska Native women and men: 2010 findings from the national intimate partner and sexual violence survey.* U.S. Department of Justice, National Institute of Justice. https://www.ojp.gov/pdffiles1/nij/249736.pdf.

Rosay, A. B. (2021). National survey estimates of violence against American Indian and Alaska Native people. *Department of Justice Journal of*

Federal Law and Practice, 69(1), 91–102. https://www.justice.gov/usao /page/file/1362691/download.

Ross, R. J. (2014). *Native American cultural participation and Post-Traumatic Stress Symptom Reduction* (1705). [Master's thesis, University of North Dakota] *Theses and Dissertations.* https://commons.und.edu/theses/1705.

Ross, R. J. (2018). *American Indian biculturalism inventory—Pueblo* (2237) [Doctoral dissertation, University of North Dakota]. *Theses and Dissertations.* https://commons.und.edu/theses/2327.

Ross, R. J., & GreyWolf, I. (2020). Indian country and COVID-19. Public Service Psychology. https://www.apadivisions.org/division-18 /publications/newsletters/public-service/2020/12/covid-indian-country.

Ross, R. J., GreyWolf, I., Smalley, K. B., & Warren, J. C. (2020). American Indian and Alaska Native health equity. In K. B. Smalley, J. C. Warren, & M. I. Fernandez (Eds.), *Health equity: A solutions-focused approach.* Springer Publishing Company.

Ross, R. J., GreyWolf, I., Tehee, M., Henry, S. M., & Cheromiah, M. (2018). Missing and murdered Indigenous women and girls. *Society of Indian Psychologists.* https://doi.org/10.17605/OSF.IO/4KMNS.

Rovner, J. (2016). Racial disparities in youth commitments and arrests: The Sentencing Project. https://www.sentencingproject.org/publications /racial-disparities-in-youth-commitments-and-arrests/.

Rushforth, E. (2020, June 15). ACLU responds to reports that Lovelace Hospital profiled pregnant Native American mothers, separated them from their newborns. ACLU of New Mexico. https://www.aclu-nm.org /en/press-releases/aclu-responds-reports-lovelace-hospital-profiled -pregnant-native-american-mothers.

Sakiestewa Gilbert, M. (2018). *Hopi Runners: Crossing the terrain between Indian and American.* University Press of Kansas.

Sando, J. S. (1992). *Pueblo nations: Eight centuries of Pueblo Indian history* (1st ed.). Clear Light Publishing.

Sargent, E. M. (2020). Resiliency as a moderating factor for the impact of adverse childhood experiences on substance use in American Indian and Caucasian college students. *Theses and Dissertations.* 3296. https:// commons.und.edu/theses/3296 [Doctoral dissertation, University of North Dakota].

Sargent, E. S. (2017). Examining drinking motivation, resiliency, and alcohol use among American Indian and Caucasian college students. *Theses and Dissertations.* 2333. https://commons.und.edu/theses/2333 [Masters thesis, University of North Dakota].

Schwing, E., Sankin, A., & Corey, M. (2018, December 17). These priests abused in Native villages for years. They retired on Gonzaga's campus. Reveal. https://revealnews.org/article/these-priests-abused-in-native -villages-for-years-they-retired-on-gonzagas-campus/.

Shores, T. (2020, May 21). Statement of United States Attorney Trent Shores, Northern District of Oklahoma, before the President's

Commission on Law Enforcement and the Administration of Justice. United States Department of Justice. https://www.justice.gov/usao-ndok /pr/statement-united-states-attorney-trent-shores-northern-district -oklahoma-president-s.

Shuey, C., Lewis, J., Keyanna, T., & Gaco, J. (2020, December 10). *Living with uranium: The impact of uranium mining on Indigenous communities* [Webinar]. Harvard Kennedy School. https://www.belfercenter.org /event/living-uranium-impact-uranium-mining-indigenous -communities.

Silovsky, J. F., Burris, L. J., McElroy, E., BigFoot, D. S., & Bonner, B. L. (2005). Honoring children, respectful ways (Treatment for Native children with sexual behavior problems). Training and treatment manuals. Indian Country Child Trauma Center, University of Oklahoma Health Sciences Center.

Simmons, D. E. (2014). *Improving the well-being of American Indian and Alaska Native children and families through state-level efforts to improve Indian Child Welfare Act compliance.* First Focus State Policy Advocacy and Reform Center. https://www.nicwa.org/wp-content/uploads/2016 /11/Improving-the-Well-being-of-American-Indian-and-Alaska-Native -Children-and-Families.pdf.

Sims, C. P. (2020). Bilingual Education in Pueblo Country. In R. B. Martinez & M.J.H. Lopez (Eds.), *The shoulders we stand on: A history of bilingual education in New Mexico* (pp. 55–76). University of New Mexico Press.

Slater, S., & Yarbrough, F. A. (2012). *Gender and sexuality in Indigenous North America: 1400–1850.* University of South Carolina Press.

Smith, R. R. (2017). Enhancing tribal sovereignty by protecting Indian civil rights: A win-win for Indian tribes and tribal members. *American Indian Law Journal* (1), 41–55. http://digitalcommons.law.seattleu.edu/ailj/vol0 /iss1/4.

Snipp, M., & Saraff, A. (2011). American Indian and Alaska Native children and families: Social and economic conditions. In M. C. Sarche, P. Spicer, P. Farrell, & H. E. Fitzgerald (Eds.), *American Indian and Alaska Native children and mental health: Development, context, prevention, and treatment* (pp. 27–42). ABC-CLIO.

Society of Indian Psychologists. (2017). *Stephen C., a minor, by Frank C., guardian ad litem, et al. v. Bureau of Indian Education, et al., Attorneys for Amicus Curiae Society of Indian Psychologists.* https://www.native psychs.org/_files/ugd/6c5978_f69e81118ff442cf87b7afb3d492e625 .pdf.

Society of Indian Psychologists. (2019). Response and recommendations for the displaying of spiritual and cultural symbols on graduation regalia for American Indian, Alaska Native, and Native Hawaiian Students. https://60a73858-fd8d-431a-89df-8d957fe23d9b.filesusr.com/ugd/6c5978 _a6d7f2c140184e71adcod95b657aobof.pdf.

Suina, M. (2017). Research is a pebble in my shoe. In E. S. Hauman & B. McK., J. Brayboy (Eds.), *Indigenous innovations in higher education: Local knowledge and critical research* (pp. 83–100). Sense Publishers.

Sumida Huaman, E., Martin, N. D., & Chosa, C. T. (2016). "Stay with your words": Indigenous youth, local policy, and the work of language fortification. *Education Policy Analysis Archives, 24*(52), 1–29. https://doi.org/10.14507/epaa.24.2346.

Sumida Huaman, E., & Stokes, P. (2011). Indigenous language revitalization and new media: Postsecondary students as innovators. *Global Media Journal, 11*(18). https://www.globalmediajournal.com/open-access/indigenous-language-revitalization-and-new-media-postsecondary-students-as-innovators.php?aid=35336&view=mobile.

Supreme Court of the Unites States. (2020). McGirt v. Oklahoma Certiorari to the Court of Criminal Appeals of Oklahoma. https://www.supremecourt.gov/opinions/19pdf/18-9526_9okb.pdf.

Swinomish Tribal Mental Health Project. (1991). *A gathering of wisdoms tribal mental health: A cultural perspective.* Swinomish Indian Tribal Community.

Swisher, K. G., & Tippeconnic, J. W. (1999). Research to support improved practice in Indian education. In K. G. Swisher & J. W. Tippeconnic, (Eds.), *Next steps: Research and practice to advance Indian education* (pp. 295–307). Eric Clearinghouse.

Tafoya, N., & Del Vecchio, A. (2005). Back to the future: An examination of the Native American holocaust experience. In M. McGoldrick, J. Giordana, & N. Garcia-Preto (Eds.), *Ethnicity and family therapy* (3rd ed., pp. 55–63). Guilford Press.

Tehee, M., & Esqueda, C. W. (2008). American Indian and European American women's perceptions of domestic violence. *Journal of Family Violence, 23*, 25–35. https://doi.org/10.1007/s10896-007-9126-7.

Tehee, M., & Green, J. (2017). Native Americans and gender. In K. Nadal (Ed.), *The SAGE encyclopedia of psychology and gender* (pp. 1225–1228). Sage Publications.

Tehee, M., Ross, R. J., McCloskey, C., & GreyWolf, I. (2021). Trauma-informed, culturally relevant psychological responses in cases of missing or murdered Indigenous peoples. *Department of Justice Journal of Federal Law and Practice, 69*(2), 251–263. https://www.justice.gov/usao/page/file/1383296/download.

Terrill, M. (2018, May 9). ASU's second Pueblo Indian doctoral cohort puts community first. *Arizona State University news.* https://asunow.asu.edu/20180509-solutions-community-first-second-pueblo-indian-cohort.

The Sentencing Project. (2020). Fact Sheet: Incarcerated women and girls. https://www.sentencingproject.org/publications/incarcerated-women-and-girls/.

Thomas, D. H. (2000). *Skull wars.* Basic Books.

Tonemah, S. A. (1991). Philosophical perspectives of gifted and talented

American Indian education. *Journal of American Indian Education, 31*(1), 3–9. https://www.jstor.org/stable/24398072.

Trahant, M. (2011, April 12). Bringing stories of abuse in Alaska into the light. https://www.indianz.com/News/2011/001105.asp.

Ullrich, J. S. (2019). For the love of our children: An Indigenous connectedness framework. *AlterNative: An International Journal of Indigenous Peoples, 15*(2), 121–130. https://doi.org/10.1177/1177180119828114.

U.S. Census. (2012). American Indian and Alaska heritage month: November 2012. https://www.census.gov/newsroom/releases/pdf/cb12ff-22_aian.pdf.

U.S. Code. (n.d.). https://uscode.house.gov/view.xhtml?path=/prelim@title34/subtitle4/chapter413&edition=prelim.

U.S. Department of Health and Human Services, Health Resources and Services Administration, Maternal and Child Health Bureau. (2013). *The health and well-being of American Indian and Alaska Native children: Parental report from the national survey of children's health, 2007.* U.S. Department of Health and Human Services.

U.S. Department of Health & Human Services, Administrative for Children and Families, Administration on Children, Youth and Families, Children's Bureau. (2018). *Child maltreatment 2018.* https://www.acf.hhs.gov/cb/research-data-technology/statistics-research/child-maltreatment.

U.S. Department of Justice, U.S. Attorney's Office. (2021, January 27). South Dakota and Montana teams that convicted former IHS doctor for serial abuse of Native American Children honored with Attorney General's Award. United States Department of Justice. https://www.justice.gov/usao-sd/pr/south-dakota-and-montana-teams-convicted-former-ihs-doctor-serial-abuse-native-american.

U.S. Government Accountability Office. (1976, November 4). Investigation of allegations concerning Indian Health Service, HRD-77-3. https://www.gao.gov/products/HRD-77-3; https://www.gao.gov/assets/120/117355.pdf.

Verney, S. P., Bennett, J., & Hamilton, J. M. (2016). Cultural considerations in the neuropsychological assessment of American Indians/Alaska Natives. In F. R. Ferraro, (Ed.)., *Minority and cross-cultural aspects of neuropsychological assessment: Enduring and emerging trends* (pp. 115–158). Taylor & Francis. https://psycnet.apa.org/record/2015-36377-011.

Wallis, V. (2002). *Raising ourselves a Gwitch'in coming of age story from the Yukon River.* Epicenter Press, Inc.

Walls, M. L., Gonzalez, J., Gladney, T., & Onello, E. (2015). Unconscious biases: Racial microaggressions in American Indian health care. *Journal of the American Board of Family Medicine, 28*(2), 231–239. https://doi.org/10.3122/jabfm.2015.02.140194.

Walters, J., & Blasing, M. (2021). AMBER Alert in Indian Country. *Department of Justice Journal of Federal Law and Practice, 69*(1), 21–34. https://www.justice.gov/usao/page/file/1362691/download.

Walters, K. L., Simoni, J. M., & Evans-Campbell, T. (2002). Substance use among American Indians and Alaska Natives: Incorporating culture in an "indigenist" stress-coping paradigm. *Public Health Reports, 117*(Suppl 1), S104-S117. https://www.ncbi.nlm.nih.gov/pmc/articles /PMC1913706/.

Warne, D., & Lajimodiere, D. (2015). American Indian health disparities: Psychosocial influences. *Social & Personality Psychology Compass, 9*(10), 567–579. https://doi.org/10.1111/spc3.12198.

Warne, D. [University of Washington School of Public Health]. (2019, April 19). Impact of unresolved trauma on American Indian health equity [Webinar]. YouTube. https://www.youtube.com/watch?v =fS7WKxDtkwY.

Warne, D. [Harvard University Native American Program]. (2021, February 7). Impact of unresolved trauma on American Indian health equity [Webinar]. YouTube. https://www.youtube.com/watch?v =CBKiKuVtrtg.

Washburn, D. (2018, April 5). How a tiny Native American community's trauma might impact education law. EdSource Highlighting Strategies for Student Success. https://edsource.org/2018/how-a-tiny-native -american-communitys-trauma-might-impact-education-law/595719.

Weaver, C., & Frosch, D. (2020, February 13). U.S. Indian Health Service doctor indicted on charges of sexual abuse. *Frontline.* https://www.pbs .org/wgbh/frontline/article/u-s-indian-health-service-doctor-indicted -on-charges-of-sexual-abuse/.

Weaver, H. N. (2001). Indigenous identity what is it, and who really has it? *American Indian Quarterly, 25*(2), 240–255. doi:10.1353/aiq.2001.0030.

Wesch, D., & Lutzker, J. R. (1991). A comprehensive 5-year evaluation of Project 12-Ways: An ecobehavioral program for treating and preventing child abuse and neglect. *Journal of Family Violence, 6*(1), 17–35. https:// doi.org/10.1007/BF00978524.

Wildcat, D. R. (2001). The schizophrenic nature of western metaphysics. In V. Deloria, Jr. & D. R. Wildcat (Eds.), *Power and place: Indian education in America* (pp. 47–55). Fulcrum Publishing. https:// nycstandswithstandingrock.files.wordpress.com/2016/10/vine-deloria-jr -daniel-r-wildcat-power-and-place-indian-education-in-america.pdf.

Wilkins, D. (2004). Justice Thomas and federal Indian law—Hitting his stride? In J. Barriero and T. Johnson (Eds.), *America is Indian country: Opinions and perspectives from Indian country today* (pp. 90–92). Fulcrum Publishing.

Willeto A.A.A. (2014). Well-being indicators for Native American children. In A. C. Michalos (Eds.), *Encyclopedia of quality of life and well-being research.* Springer, Dordrecht. https://doi.org/10.1007/978-94-007-0753 -5_3774.

Willis, D. J., DeLeon, P. H., Haldane, S., & Heldring, M. B. (2014). A policy article—Personal perspectives on the public policy process: Making a difference. *Professional Psychology: Research and Practice, 45*(2), 143. https://doi.org/10.1037/a0036234.

Willis, D. J., & Spicer, P. (2013). American Indian and Alaska Native children and families. In A. McDonald Culp (Ed.), *Child and family advocacy: Bridging the gaps between research, practice, and policy* (pp. 191–201). Springer Science + Business Media. https://doi.org/10 .1007/978-1-4614-7456-2_13.

Wilson, S. (2007). Guest editorial: What is an Indigenist research paradigm? *Canadian Journal of Native Education, 30*(2), 193–195. Edmonton.

Winters, K. C., & Winters, M. K. (2020). Secondary trauma: The unintended consequence of trauma. *Prevention in Our Native American Communities, 1*(3), 3–9. https://pttcnetwork.org/sites/default/files/2020 -07/Prev%20Vol%201%20Issue%203%20Summer%202020.pdf.

Wolsko, C., Lardon, C., Mohatt, G. V., & Orr, E. (2007). Stress, coping, and well-being among the Yupik of the Yukon-Kuskokwim Delta: The role of enculturation and acculturation. *International Journal of Circumpolar Health, 66*(1), 51–61. https://doi.org/10.3402/ijch.v66i1.18226.

Zion, J. W. (1998). The dynamics of Navajo peacemaking. *Journal of Contemporary Criminal Justice, 14*(1), 58–74. https://doi.org/10.1177 /1043986298014001005.

Index

adverse childhood experience (ACEs), 46, 67, 71–73, 97
alcohol-attributable deaths (AAD), 71
assimilation, 31, 40, 65, 66, 123, 125

banishment, 20, 126
Bigfoot, Dolores Subia, 9–10, 15, 120
boarding school: cultural assimilation, 32, 70, 123; experience, 11–12, 33–35; forced, 23, 93; language, 63; propaganda, 86; trauma, 45, 65, 72, 132
Brayboy, Bryan McKinley Jones: adjust, 58; altruism, 62; education, 65–66, 95, 133; extended family, 13–14; practice, 120; statistics, 40; TribalCrit, 55

Cheromiah, M., 17, 38
child-rearing, 10
collectivistic: communitarianism, 30; contradiction, 110; giving back, 21–22; intelligence, 23; orientation, 9–10, 17, 19, 77, 120, 132; trauma, 58
colonialism, 6, 63–66, 70
communitarianism, 25, 30
connectedness, 52–53, 62, 99
cultural genocide, 26, 31–32, 130
cultural humility, 71, 73, 109, 136

culturally competent, 73, 136
culturally relevant: detention center, 99; strengths, 54; treatment, 73, 103, 109–110, 128, 136

Dakota Access Pipeline, 42, 127
data: ACEs, 72; disparity, 43–44, 83, 111; efforts, 134, 136; statistics, 79, 98; stereotype, 112–113

educational system: assimilated, 37, 39, 63; maltreatment, 32, 97; systematic, 30, 65; tribe, 16, 94
elders: child maltreatment, 30, 103; children, 10, 24; law, 19, 74, 77–78, 96; respect, 9, 108; upbringing, 12, 14, 137; violence, 35, 49, 137
encouragement, 74, 120
environmental trauma, 127–129
experimentation, 34–35, 93
extended family, 9–14, 59, 61, 100, 107

giving back, 21–22
Gone, Joseph P., 12, 16, 21, 31, 51, 120
GreyWolf, Iva, 11–12, 34–35, 51, 120

historical trauma: ACEs, 67, 72; federal government, 79, 96; implications, 123–124; our voices, 9; youth, 50
humor, 4, 11, 18–19

About the Authors

ROYLEEN J. ROSS, PHD, is tribally enrolled at the Pueblo of Laguna, in New Mexico. She is employed as a cultural psychologist and deputy director at a regional southwest tribal organization. Dr. Ross has coauthored book chapters on American Indian and Alaska Native Health Equity and Cognitive Behavior Therapy for Depression with American Indians. She is involved in other projects related to the intersectionality between mental health and law enforcement in Indian Country, attributed in part to her former career experience as an FBI Agent and New Mexico State Policeman. Her professional interests include policy development, social justice, health equity, advocacy at the tribal, state, and federal levels, and the advancement of mental health for Indigenous Peoples.

JULII M. GREEN (African American & Eastern Band Cherokee) is from San Diego, California. She is an associate professor in the Clinical Psychology PsyD Department at CSPP/AIU-San Diego where she teaches Foundations in multicultural psychology, Family Therapy with Ethnic Families, Qualitative Research Methods, and Practicum Consultation. Her scholarship focuses on allyship, activism, social determinants of health, and the impact of IPV on Native women as well as their families, and she has authored peer-reviewed articles and book chapters dealing with the aforementioned subjects. Green is also a therapist within the community, focusing on ethnically diverse clients, navigating systemic racism, and mental health concerns. Additionally, she serves on department, local, and national psychological committees addressing equity, diversity, inclusion, sexism, and systemic racism.

MILTON A. FUENTES is a professor of psychology at Montclair State University in Montclair, New Jersey, and a licensed psychologist in New Jersey and New York. His scholarship focuses on equity, diversity, and inclusion; and he has authored several peer-reviewed articles, book chapters, and books dealing with the aforementioned subjects. Fuentes also coauthored a manual with Julia Silva for facilitators of the ACT Raising Safe Kids Program, an international parenting program housed at the American Psychological Association. In this manual, he applies the principles of motivational interviewing to the program's parenting sessions, promoting child welfare, and discouraging child maltreatment.

THE PREVENTING CHILD MALTREATMENT COLLECTION

PREVENTING CHILD MALTREATMENT IN THE U.S.	PREVENTING CHILD MALTREATMENT IN THE U.S.	PREVENTING CHILD MALTREATMENT IN THE U.S.	PREVENTING CHILD MALTREATMENT IN THE U.S.
MULTICULTURAL CONSIDERATIONS	THE LATINX COMMUNITY PERSPECTIVE	AMERICAN INDIAN AND ALASKA NATIVE PERSPECTIVES	THE BLACK COMMUNITY PERSPECTIVE
MILTON A. FUENTES RACHEL R. SINGER RENEE L. DEBOARD-LUCAS	ESTHER J. CALZADA MONICA FAULKNER CATHERINE A. LABRENZ MILTON A. FUENTES	ROYLEEN J. ROSS JULII M. GREEN MILTON A. FUENTES	MELISSA PHILLIPS SHAVONNE J. MOORE-LOBBAN MILTON A. FUENTES
PREVENTING CHILD MALTREATMENT IN THE U.S.: MULTICULTURAL CONSIDERATIONS Milton A. Fuentes, Rachel R. Singer, and Renee L. DeBoard-Lucas 9781978822573 **Paper** 9781978822580 **Cloth**	**PREVENTING CHILD MALTREATMENT IN THE U.S.: THE LATINX COMMUNITY PERSPECTIVE** Esther J. Calzada, Monica Faulkner, Catherine LaBrenz, and Milton A. Fuentes 9781978822887 **Paper** 9781978822894 **Cloth**	**PREVENTING CHILD MALTREATMENT IN THE U.S.: AMERICAN INDIAN AND ALASKA NATIVE PERSPECTIVES** Royleen J. Ross, Julii M. Green, and Milton A. Fuentes 9781978821101 **Paper** 9781978821118 **Cloth**	**PREVENTING CHILD MALTREATMENT IN THE U.S.: THE BLACK COMMUNITY PERSPECTIVE** Melissa Phillips, Shavonne J. Moore-Lobban, and Milton A. Fuentes 9781978820630 **Paper** 9781978820647 **Cloth**

The Preventing Child Maltreatment collection is a four-book miniseries within the Violence Against Women and Children series at Rutgers University Press. This collection, curated by Milton A. Fuentes from Montclair State University, is devoted to advancing an understanding of the dynamics of child maltreatment across ethnically diverse populations. Starting with *Preventing Child Maltreatment in the U.S.: Multicultural Considerations*, which provides a general examination of child maltreatment through the interaction of feminist, multicultural, and social justice lenses, the rest of the series takes a closer look at Native American/Alaska Native, Black, and Latinx communities in order to provide insight for social workers who may encounter those populations within their scope of treatment. Policymakers, practitioners, graduate students, and social workers of all kinds will find this collection of great interest.

 RUTGERSUNIVERSITYPRESS
rutgersuniversitypress.org

Printed in the United States
by Baker & Taylor Publisher Services